TEACHERS CHANGE LIVES 24/7

150 ways to do it right...

Jim Burgett

Including the best from Jim's most sought presentation:

*"How to be an Effective Teacher, Remain Sane,
And Stay Out of Jail—all at the Same Time!*

First printing, March 2007
Second printing, April 2007
Third printing, September, 2007
Fourth printing, January, 2008

Cover by Douglas Burgett

ISBN 0910167915

Also available in .PDF format: ISBN 0910167109

Table of Contents

AUTHOR'S BIOGRAPHY

JIM BURGETT

Jim Burgett is a veteran educator, speaker, presenter, consultant, and author. He has taught at the elementary, junior high, high school, and college levels, and been a principal at the first three. Burgett was Superintendent of the Elizabeth and River Ridge School Districts in northwestern Illinois and the Highland Community Unit School District in Illinois, near St. Louis.

During Jim's superintendency at Highland, the high school earned the Blue Ribbon Award from the U.S. Department of Education and had one of the highest percentages of nationally board certified teachers in the nation.

The Illinois and American Association of School Administrators named Burgett the Illinois Superintendent of the Year. He was also named Administrator of the Year by the Illinois Association of Educational Office Professionals. In addition, Jim was a Teacher of the Year and earned many other special awards during his career for his leadership.

Jim is a consultant, presenter, and speaker for many professional associations across the country. His message is one of common sense, practical information, and inspiration. He is much sought for annual conferences because of his insights, ability to touch the heart and tickle the funny bone, and practical suggestions on what to do *right now* to improve the future. Burgett's goal as an educator has always been to make a difference for kids, and his leadership as a facilitator, presenter, or speaker is based on the same goal.

Jim currently leads the Burgett Group, a company providing professional development services. He facilitates strategic planning, provides educational workshops and motivational presentations, and has served on a variety of local, state, and national boards, committees, and task forces.

Burgett's first book, ***What Every Superintendent and Principal Needs to Know***, is a national best seller just released in its second edition. In addition to this book (***Teachers Change Lives 24/7***), Jim co-authored ***The Perfect School***, also published in 2007.

He has helped many school districts, colleges, and professional organizations craft their own strategic plans. Jim writes and presents administrator academies and also appears frequently as a guest speaker at colleges and universities.

After a lifetime of teaching, coaching, leading, and passionately working to make a difference, Jim has pulled together material from his many presentations, his personal experiences in education, and his files of information obtained from other educators to write ***Teachers Make a Difference 24/7***.

Burgett is an educator who wants to make a difference.

DEDICATION

I dedicate this work of love to kids.

First, to our three children. Each of you have made your mom and me so proud we can hardly stand it.

Then to their kids. As I write this, there are five of them. They range from preschool to sixth grade, from dance class to basketball, from bubbling excitement to pre-teen craziness. The fact that they will all be in school next year spurs me to work even harder to encourage teachers to make a positive difference. Who doesn't want their children (or grandchildren) to have the very best teachers available? Who doesn't think they deserve the very best?

Finally, to all kids. This book is dedicated to you, the reason why most of us entered the profession of teaching in the first place. We didn't do it for the money. We did it because we love kids; we want to change you positively. Teachers change lives, and their influence is 24/7. This book was written for you, so that teachers just might be motivated or encouraged to make an even greater difference in your lives.

ACKNOWLEDGMENTS

Over the years so many have influenced and helped me that it would be impossible to give credit where credit is due. To those I have not listed, please know that your contribution toward crafting this work of love is real and appreciated.

To Gordon Burgett, the eldest of the Burgett siblings by six minutes, I can't thank you enough for your support. I wouldn't be an author without your guidance and encouragement. I can't count how many times you have told me you are proud of my work as an educator. Your words mean a lot. I have *always* been proud of you.

To my wife since 1967. How lucky can a guy be to marry the girl he fell in love with in junior high? Three kids and lots of grandchildren later, I still love you just as much. The peace and happiness you provided at home allowed me to be a better teacher and person. I am indeed one lucky guy.

To the teachers and educators I have been blessed to know and work with over the years. From Elizabeth to Highland, from across Illinois to across the United States, I have met and worked with some of the very best. I have learned from you. You do change lives 24/7.

To the Boards of Education that allowed me to stumble, to experiment, to lead, to teach, and to share. A few of you have left this earth, folks like Ken, Karen, and Harold, but you will never leave my heart. To Darell, Wayne, and Terry —you were the best Board Presidents ever, and each became wonderful personal friends. I thank you for your leadership, and for letting me grow.

And to my faith in God. There are many times when I need help and guidance. My minister or my church partners are always there. Nothing was more helpful than having the freedom to pray. He is always waiting to help. He is with me 24/7.

Other publications by Jim Burgett

◆ *The Perfect School* (2007)
◆ *What Every Superintendent and Principal Needs to Know* (2nd ed., 2007)
◆ "How to Handle the Death of a Student, Faculty, or Staff Member" (2004)

For more information about E.C.U. products, see the page at the end of this book and/or check the website at www.superintendents-and-principals.com.

Introduction

I knew Jim before he knew himself. The first time I saw him he was naked, puckered, and wailing. With an appearance and temperament like that, I figured he'd survive about two miserable years. I was eight and he was my kid brother.

Now he's written his own book, every last word. Go figure.

It's a good book, too. He's a funny guy and that seeps through on every page. But mostly Jim is a teacher, and by extension a storyteller. So, on these pages Jim mainly tells stories. He tells about Mr. Ruggles, Mr. B, Mike Klippert, Paula Shea, and a dozen or two more. His heroes, who turn out to be remarkably like Jim himself.

They are all excellent teachers and great leaders, champions to kids and blessings to parents. They are the prototypes of what Jim wants all teachers to see and emulate because, as his title says, *Teachers Change Lives 24/7*—and that's too big a responsibility to give to anybody who doesn't flat-out love kids and want to help open up an exciting new world to them.

In fact, Jim says it best in one of the 175 ways by which teachers might excel in their life-changing quest:

> *If you don't love kids, love your job, and love the field of education, quit. Liking isn't good enough when it comes to children's lives.*

I became involved in Jim's literary pursuits nearly five years ago when he and two of his cronies, Drs. Max McGee and Jim Rosborg (themselves top leaders in Illinois education) asked me a question about publishing a book they were writing together. I so liked the idea and the wisdom the three imparted, my publishing firm bid on their brainchild, and that became *What Every Superintendent and Principal Needs to Know*. It rightly became a best seller (with the second, revised edition being released in 2007). The same three are presently finishing another dandy book on educational administration called *The Perfect School* (also a 2007 release).

All along, Jim has been wooing educational audiences with speeches, keynotes, and strategic planning sessions, and in the process has created his own, unique pool of wisdom, laced with laughter and more than a few tears, all told through stories about the best teachers, how to solve problems immediately, and how to make the school a hallowed hall from which only good things emerge.

So I asked the kid when I could share that information with you too, so many more of you could hear his words and thoughts. This book is the result.

It's a grand offering and he's done the odd Burgett family proud again. But you decide...

(If you want to see what others think of the book, check www.superintendents-and-principals.com).

Gordon Burgett
Publisher, Education Communication Unlimited

Chapter One

The Journey

Why don't we take a journey together? Let's travel, through this book, into many hamlets of education. There will even be a prize at the end—you will have new tools to help you become a more effective teacher, a better person, and a stronger, positive influence on others.

These pages are written as much from my heart as my head. It's not a research manual so it won't quote a score of famous authors, nor will it give you a rigid or even exact formula for teaching success. What it will do is suggest a useful mix of ideas, thoughts, experiences, and tools.

It's based on actual happenings, shared processes, witnessed successes (and failures), readings, and other sources. And it's really not my book, but our book. I say that because teachers are bound together by commonly-shared elements, one of which is a desire to make a difference in this world.

Still, it starts with me and the 61 years I have been preparing the mix. That's how long I've been in education.

Before you panic and think I'm a Geritol-guggling senior citizen writing from the sunroom of a rest home, let me add some additional facts to consider. My involvement in education began at birth. From the outset I was the recipient of non-stop education: how to eat, when to sleep, how to laugh (my brothers were tickle freaks), what to wear (mostly cloth diapers), how to communicate when Dad would accidentally poke me with a diaper pin, and lots more.

In year two, give or take a few months, I learned how to walk, talk, express my thoughts, and try new things. I figured out when to please and when to agitate. I even learned new ways of communication, with crayons and letters and books.

From then on, I was on a ballistic learning curve: running in circles, reading, riding bikes, adding and subtracting, singing songs, swinging a bat, swimming...

There was always someone there to teach me something—one of my two older brothers (twins, who were eight when I was born), my dad, my mom, a neighbor, or a friend. Sometimes what I learned was inappropriate, at which point I learned what inappropriate meant and I had to decide whether I wanted to continue to be inappropriate (with its consequences) or not. That's all part of it.

By five, I was in kindergarten. Many think that learning begins when we enter school. Research tells us that we have learned a high percentage of what we will ever learn before we walk through those magic doors on that fateful first day (watched by a weeping or joyful Mom). *All I Really Need to Know I Learned in Kindergarten* shares the importance of those first few years.

I learned that being cute with big brown eyes and an angelic smile got me more favors than some of my friends, who were loud, obnoxious, or even evil.

In my youth, preschool meant staying at home with a mom who didn't "have a job." Still to be invented were multi-folded, plastic, high tech diapers with Velcro and pictures of action figures. We suffered through Dreft and a pail filled with obnoxiously smelly, used cotton squares.

We didn't wash our hands as often as we do now and we probably didn't know all the correct ways to prepare food. We drank thick, cream-laden milk (sometimes mixed with chocolate powder) and we ate real butter, not "It's Almost Butter" or "Fooled You—This Really is Plastic Butter!" And white bread. We would never pay for water when it came free from the tap.

We let our marshmallows get crispy black at the campfire and never once thought about carcinogens. Fiber was what they used to make rope, and we pulled apples off trees and ate them regardless of their color or cleanliness. I'm not sure if those were the "good old days," but, for good or bad, we survived.

We even sat two feet away from the television set. Of course the screen was 12" across and had a strange circle-like shape. What we saw was black and white and, at best, fuzzy. "Howdy Doody" came on at 4:30. The "Friday Night Fights" were a big attraction. There were no computers, no cell phones, no digital cameras, no air conditioning in cars (except lowered windows), no fast foods, and no microwaves. Your head was your calculator. Your dictionary was your spell checker. The *Encyclopedia Britannica*, sold by a guy who came door-to-door, was your reference source. (Some bought their encyclopedias at the grocery store one volume a week.) Your bike had one gear, fat tires, a big seat, and it came with fenders that most boys removed within minutes. And everything you did had to do with education. Every experience, every communication, every relationship added to your kit of knowledge.

In school I learned so much I couldn't begin to write it down, nor did I know I should. But here, five or six decades later, I will share some of those school-related stories that changed my life and modeled the way I have hopefully changed the lives of others. I'm sharing them now because I suspect that some of these examples still work today.

My education was more "formal" from about five to twenty two. I breezed through the first twelve years in about twelve years. I wasn't the valedictorian, but I did make it to the National Honor Society. I don't recall being named student of the day, student of the week, student of the month, or student of the year. But then again, I don't remember spending any days in detention, suspended, expelled, or sentenced for anything. (I did get my share of speeding tickets, but that's another story.)

Nonetheless, I managed to escape juvenile saintliness. There was that time in junior high when I was a guest of the principal—but it wasn't my fault! And the time I kicked my fifth grade teacher—once. My mom then kicked me full of instant respect, took away about every privilege I thought I had, and made me pay a big price for my behavior. I learned a lot from that one kick.

Life in school was full of learning, but unlike most other kids, from sixth grade on that learning expanded to new fronts with a suddenly mixed up, challenging, and confusing home life.

I was learning how to process what a wide variety of teachers were teaching me, including coaches, mentors, Sunday School teachers, Boy Scout leaders, and anybody who was so inclined to help me grow intellectually, physically, and spiritually. Unknowingly, I was also learning *how to teach*. From the day I met Mr. Ruggles I studied teachers as much as what they taught. Mr. Ruggles made me *want* to teach. (Let's save Mr. Ruggles for the next chapter.)

From high school I went directly to the University of Illinois. I used to visit my brother Gordon who was a student there. He was 22 then and I was about 14. I loved the visits and the Champaign-Urbana campus. It was at the U. of I. that I planned to become a teacher, or so I thought.

But, like lots of other students, I had to work a lot when I got there and, while I was smart enough, my time management skills were pretty dumb. So at the end of three semesters I had exactly a "C" average. Decision time: my GPA was too low for admission into the College of Education. I could either change majors or change my life. I chose the later.

For one semester I went to work in a factory. I scored too high on the application exams to do piecework in the big building so they put me in the office—as a time management specialist. Me, a time management specialist? Didn't they know it was my lack of time management skills that got me to the factory in the first place! I had to wear a tie and jacket and I earned less than the guys in the factory. Yet in other ways I learned many of life's most profound lessons. One, I saw first hand the difference between those who were dedicated to their work versus those solely dedicated to a paycheck. Two, I couldn't wait to get back to becoming a teacher.

With new vigor and a bit of my newly-found time management specialization, the next three years were super. I transferred to the University of Wisconsin, in Platteville. I married the girl I fell in love with during eighth grade but didn't seriously date until college. I learned how to juggle 40 to 60 hours of work each week on top of my schooling, and I discovered a new work ethic: I never earned less than an A from then until I had finished my third degree.

I grew up. I put into place what others had shared with me. I was serious about a career, a marriage, and my life.

I still have the same wonderful wife and I'm just retired from education as a teacher, principal, and superintendent, taking the last position in my early thirties. I've continued to provide professional development for educators, something I have been doing for about 20 years. And I've miraculously become an author. I've been blessed in many, many ways, and I'm still learning…

A couple more thoughts before we start our journey. My experience as an educator has allowed me to teach students from fifth grade to graduate school. I spent the majority of my years teaching the hormonally-challenged middle schoolers. Many suggest that you need a lobotomy to teach this age group. If I had one, I can't remember it. I actually love that age and still teach fifteen students each week from grades 7-12 in a Sunday School class.

I have also worked in districts with thousands of kids, and some with only a few hundred. I have worked with national leaders and local councils; I've witnessed poverty and affluence. I have fought for adequate resources, built new schools, and watched students become exceptional contributors to society. I have also buried far too many students, far too young.

My experiences in the classroom and as an administrator at all levels in the public school system have allowed me to work with some of the most talented, and most frightening, educators one might meet. Each educator, along with every student and family I have encountered and every experience I have lived through, have helped write this book.

So, with that said, I promise you my best effort. Please understand that I will knowingly change a few names here and there, mostly because I'm not sure if the folks would want true-name exposure in this sure-to-be national best seller, but I will stick to the facts as much as my mind allows.

Finally, this book is a way to share with you what many have so graciously shared with me. I am writing it from a lifetime of passion doing what I love. I truly hope that, in some small way, it instills in you that same passion.

Let's start the journey!

Chapter Two

Mr. Ruggles

I want to introduce Mr. Ruggles, as I remember him.

His impact on me was immense. It's the same impact I've tried to have on my students and my own kids.

Sometime during the sixth grade our teacher was drafted. The principal came to our room to tell us that we would have a substitute for a while until a replacement could be found. No one cried. He was a nice guy, but he didn't shake the world. I don't even remember his name. Sadly, he was forgettable.

His substitute was a legitimate Evil Witch from the East. She had no control over us. Her tactics were bizarre. Not that we were hellions—we were a normal, middle class group of sixth graders living in the suburbs of Chicago. The boys ranged from small and underdeveloped to Bob M. Bob was six feet tall, had hair on his legs, and seemed old enough to drive the school bus. He also wore his collar turned up, which in those days made him a sort of hoodlum-in-training. The girls ranged from small, skinny things oblivious to their attire or makeup to Peggy W. Peggy was like Annette in the Mickey Mouse Club. Need I say more? When our first teacher was teaching, we were a well-behaved, fun class. When the EW arrived, our evil was also provoked.

I guess she didn't know, or remember, that students will generally meet the level of expectation you set for them. Expect them to be well behaved and you have a better chance of having well behaved kids. Give them encouragement to be

monsters (however slight) and you create monsters. We became the monsters the EW expected us to be.

I remember one time when her attempt to control conduct
by flashing the lights off and on didn't work. When she realized that we were ignoring her wattage interruptions by con-
tinuing to talk and laugh in spite of the light show, she picked
up the cowbell from her desk and threw it toward Bob M who
was in the back row. It missed him but hit the wall. Man
could she throw! Bob started to laugh, which caused us all to
laugh, so she started to cry. Then she fled, got the principal,
and he finished the day. Apparently she got on her broom and
flew home. (Why did she have a cowbell at all? To quiet us
down. It worked once.)

In retrospect, I learned a lot from the EW. I learned that
bad teachers don't earn respect. I learned that good kids can
turn nasty if allowed to. I also learned that it doesn't take a
rocket scientist to know that in order for learning to take
place, a teacher has to create a learning environment. That
includes knowing how to teach, gaining respect from the students, and setting and maintaining high expectations of behavior.

So at the start of a new day, after a couple of horrendous
weeks with the EW, we were greeted once again by the principal. Next to him stood this big, rather good-looking young
man. Teachers wore ties and coats and looked professional in
those days. The new guy looked exceptionally impressive.

"Boys and girls, this is Mr. Ruggles. He will be your new
teacher," announced the principal. At that moment my life
changed.

We were ready for a good teacher. Kids want to know
their limits, they want to be disciplined (fairly), and they want
order. Not just at school but at home, at church school, at the
YMCA swimming class, or anywhere. Good, effective teach-

ers understand this basic principle and set realistic expectations for behavior and learning. They set it from the start, then they work on it every day. They are consistent, fair, and don't waiver much.

Mr. Ruggles expected us to act like mature kids, not hideous rejects. He was firm from minute one. The first time someone spoke while he was speaking, he simply looked at that student, paused a moment, and went on. The kid got the point. No one tested him. He had what I call "eyeball discipline." He looked you into submission. I can almost hear him saying to that kid, had the kid decided to talk, "Young man, when you are asked to talk I won't interrupt you or be rude. I expect the same from you when anyone else is talking. Do you understand?" You felt that he would not tolerate inappropriate behavior. Within minutes, we were back to our old selves. We had lost one teacher to the armed services, another was elsewhere brewing the eyes of newts, and now we had Mr. Ruggles. He had us in the palm of his hand. Sometimes all it takes is confidence, demeanor, and no-nonsense comportment.

His first few words were amazing. He said he was a new teacher, that all his life he wanted to teach, that he was at a disadvantage coming in the middle of the year and not knowing us, but that he would visit each one of us at home within the next few weeks to catch up on who we were. At home! And he did it! I remember when he came to my house and had lunch with my mom and me. We learned that he had played football in college and was engaged. He charmed my mother with his polite manners.

Every morning, before school began, Mr. Ruggles was surrounded by kids. Other teachers were talking to other teachers, maybe with a coffee cup in hand, but Mr. Ruggles was talking to kids. His focus was obvious.

His dedication was most evident during the lunch break. As we finished eating, Mr. Ruggles would appear with a kickball, softball, or a basketball, and he would walk through the cafeteria announcing that anyone who wanted to play should follow him to the field or gym. He would reach down and tap a couple of kids on the shoulder and tell them he needed some help and ask them to come along. Usually these were the kids that sat by themselves and rarely went out and mingled with other kids. We knew what he was doing, and so did those kids. And it worked!

Once we were outside, he'd say he needed two teams. Then he would cleverly add something like, "Everyone with blue eyes, green eyes, or purple eyes go over here and all the brown-eyed folks line up here." Or maybe it was Catholics vs. Protestants or guys against girls (and then he would have the guys bat with their weak hand.) No matter what he did, we laughed, had fun, burned off energy, and *he made us feel good about ourselves.*

I remember one time when a not-so-athletic boy came up to bat and missed the ball by a foot with each swing. Mr. Ruggles finally said, "John, your swing is great, your skills are super, but the ball is just too small!" Everyone laughed, especially John. And then on the way inside, he walked next to John and I could see him demonstrating how to swing a bat properly.

He was something else. He made us feel like we were too. And how he handled us was a huge example of effective teaching. Never mess with someone's self esteem. Make them feel valuable. Criticize with caution, never criticizing the person, just the behavior. When you can, make them feel good while at the same time teach them to improve. Mr. Ruggles was a genius when it came to making us want to learn.

Guess what? Years later I talked to the man who was principal that first year of Mr. Ruggles' career. He shared with me that Mr. Ruggles was never assigned noontime activities. He did it on his own with no expectation of a stipend or other reward other than seeing us grow and learn. I could go on and on about Mr. Ruggles. Let me end by saying that he made you want to come to school. He made you enjoy learning. He made you feel valued. He made a difference. He changed lives. He sure changed mine.

> Here are the first of 175 things that teachers can do to change lives better. I couldn't stop at 150.

◆ Recognize students who demonstrate good citizenship. "Not everyone has the ability to be an 'A' student, but we all have the ability to become an 'A' citizen." Allow good citizens to lead the pledge, pass out papers, etc. This builds everyone's self-esteem, especially the average or struggling student who doesn't get the academic pats on the back.

◆ Meet students in the hallways. Get to know them. A middle school teacher reports, "I met lots of third graders this year because a group was collecting rocks and they would show them to me. I promised them a special rock unit when they got to my class in fifth grade. I saved some of their rocks for the unit. That will keep their interest."

◆ Maintain a positive-reinforcement self-esteem checklist. Put every student on the checklist. Make a concerted effort to compliment every student, individually, either orally or in writing, once every other day (or at least once a week). When you give a compliment, mark it on the checklist. At the end of a week, see which students you are inadvertently avoiding.

◆ Don't let any student fall through the cracks. Periodically review your class roster and mentally ask yourself if you know the student, if you are connecting with the student, and if you are meeting his or her needs.

◆ Patience, kindness, confidence, and high expectations can work wonders when establishing an environment for learning.

Chapter Three

Home Management

Teachers have two houses. One, they live in; the other is their schoolhouse.

Most teachers also have a family of sorts. They might have a spouse and maybe even kids. Or they might have a roommate or significant other. Almost everyone has a Mom, Dad, or siblings. That covers most situations.

Along with family or friends, most teachers have an actual house, apartment, or dwelling to pay for, maintain, heat, make comfortable, and live in. And all teachers have the usual daily issues to address. In short, none of us is problem-free nor do we live in a perfect house or household.

Let's lump all the above under the umbrella of "your house." That is where you live, with whom, and all the usual human issues you resolve outside of school.

In this short chapter I want you to see that your house affects the schoolhouse.

You also have a huge influence on the schoolhouse. You may think you are one small cog on a huge wheel of management and operations. You may consider yourself "just a teacher." You don't control the tax rate, public opinion, state law, or even the salary schedule. You have one vote with the association and not much contact with the "suits" that run the place. You come to the schoolhouse, do your work, and don't rattle many cages. If you think like this, you are entitled to your opinion, even though your opinion is *dead wrong*.

You are the most important part of the schoolhouse. Don't get me wrong: every person who is a part of the school system has value. But you most directly affect the lives of children. You change their lives. You are the single most important expeditor of the basic premise of schools, which is to provide the best educational opportunities for children, within the available resources. If *you* don't do that, kids are cheated. If your cog in the big wheel doesn't fit, the wheel simply doesn't turn right.

In order for you to do your job as well as possible, you must be an adroit manager of two houses. No one taught you this at the university. This was not a chapter in your education textbooks, but it may be the single most important component of your success as an educator.

You see, if you can't manage your own house, then you can't be at your best in the schoolhouse. It works the other way too. If the schoolhouse causes you to function poorly, your own house will also pay a price.

Ever go to work after a "few words" at home with someone who matters? Or did you ever go to work after a long night on the couch, or a day or two with tense (or no) communication? Ever deal with a child's problem, maybe a son up all night with jaundice or a missing daughter still out at dawn with a friend? Ever cry (or been cried at) half the night over a disagreement, or from worry? How often did you spend anxious days and nights trying to make your money last until the end of the month, or agonize about a bill, or an overdue debt, or an out-of-work partner? Ever deal with an addiction —or an addicted person you love? Whether it was alcohol, drugs, gambling, dishonesty, or infidelity, that list is long and, for most, an unwelcome guest.

It doesn't take a genius to know that if your house isn't right, you will carry it over to the schoolhouse. It's called baggage. You have to manage both houses well to provide the best learning conditions for your kids and the best living conditions for your family.

When life is good in your house, it's usually just as good in the schoolhouse. When you come to work with few cares and a positive attitude, there is little blocking your ability to focus on the needs of your school kids. When you come to the schoolhouse out of balance because of personal issues, it's hard to focus, hard to concentrate, hard to help others.

Sometimes we think that life can be easily segmented and managed on both fronts. Some folks can do that for a while, but when your professional life is as stressful as it is in education, and when so much depends on your ethical, reasonable, and intellectual abilities, it becomes almost impossible to do your best if you can't manage your own house well.

So what do you do? You take a hard look at your life. You identify your problems. You face them. You communicate them. You change them.

Of course, if it really were always that easy, we wouldn't need Dr. Phil. But it's not. It's darn hard to manage either or both houses so that life is always flowing smoothly.

I shared this very message once at a conference of administrators in Iowa. Several weeks after the conference, I received an e-mail from a lady who had attended. She began the message by saying that because of me she had divorced her husband. I felt terrible until I read a bit farther.

She said that my comments about balancing both houses made her think how unhappy they had been for years. She went home that very night and they talked. She told me that she realized that most days she went to the schoolhouse either angry or just on autopilot. She had lost her passion for teaching. She wasn't happy at school or at home. After they talked, he admitted the same thing. They decided that night that the conversation was a couple of years overdue. They also decided to divorce and move on.

She wrote to me not because I was a home wrecker but because thinking about the two houses made her discover that she was basically unhappy. She ended the e-mail by saying that she and her ex-husband had a date that night and that they hadn't been so happy in many years. She also said that her teaching was more exciting now *than ever before*.

And then she said what I think was the most important thing, that all it took was the courage to face the situation. After that, it was easy.

Do you have a situation to face? If not, then feel blessed and lucky. Keep up the good job of providing a balance between your house and the schoolhouse. If, however, something is holding you back from being and doing your best, think about it. Talk to someone who can provide honest, professional guidance, and take action. Many school districts or health insurance programs offer a service that provides help with family or personal situations. These services are almost always confidential, but it is imperative that you check before you make contact. If your school does not offer this type of "employee assistance program," they should consider it because it is one of the least expensive benefits they can provide. If you attend a church, are affiliated with a denomination, or know a friend who is, this too can be an opportunity for confidential help. Prayer, faith, belief in God, or a spiritual foundation is always a primary option to consider. Personally, it has been my basic source of strength in all situations.

Life is too short. Your kids, at home and at school, deserve the best from you—and *you* deserve the best from you as well. Balancing your house and the schoolhouse may be two of the biggest challenges you will ever face, and maybe the most important ones as well.

◆ Need a break to think or unwind? Walk the halls. Walk the halls before or after school or during your free period. A ten-minute walk will do wonders for the mind and body. No one needs to know about it either. Who will stop a walking teacher and ask you what you are doing? Stairs also help with your stamina, strength, and cardio condition.

◆ Here is a way to multiply the interest and involvement of your students at the schoolhouse. If you are used to sending newsletters home to the parents, why not get the addresses of the grandparents, ministers, or two of each student's favorite adults, and send copies to them as well (or have the students hand them out)? When you praise the students or discuss the neat things they are doing in your class, you will be giving each student a larger and stronger support base.

◆ There are dozens of ways your school can involve the community. Signboard announcements, grandparents' day, parents' night, new school orientation, welcome wagons, senior citizen volunteers, retired folks as classroom volunteers, senior citizen proms—these are just a few ways that the community can be involved with the school. You, or your class of students, can start or promote any one of these ideas and can make a difference.

◆ If you are a smoker, quit. Your actions speak far louder than your words. If you quit, you can become a role model for kids. If you have a loved one who has died from a smoking-related cause, you can share that with kids. You can change lives and maybe even save a few. And, if you do quit smoking, you can also keep living longer and healthier!

◆ Start each day with a plan and a list of things to do, not just at school but also at home. Organization leads to productivity.

◆ As a parent, never let your child leave home thinking you're angry with him. As a teacher, never let a child leave for home thinking the same thing. It's the same theory as never going to bed mad at your spouse. It's just not right. Your kids, at home and at school, need to know that you love them and care for them. Resolve issues promptly. If you can't resolve them entirely, at least let them know that no matter what is going on, you love them.

◆ You may want to go into the faculty room and tear a student apart or laugh at her. Don't do it. It won't help you or the student. The same is true at home. You may want to criticize and say things that you will regret. Work at refocusing this behavior. Take a walk outside, count to 50, call a friend and talk about another topic. Don't share anything that you may feel the need to retract later.

◆ When you go home at night after a stressful day, remember not to take it out on your family. Those are the people who love and need you the most. When you go to school in the morning, remember not to take family issues out on your students. Many of them are coming to school with family issues of their own and they are looking to you for comfort, safety, compassion, and understanding. No one said that being a teacher was a walk in the park. You are needed and important

24/7. You change lives 24/7. You have to be balanced and in control. That is why you teach. You can do it.

◆ Being a great teacher is wonderful, but not at the cost of your health, family, or sanity. Put your job in perspective. If it is getting to you, ask yourself why, then make adjustments. If you don't know why, and you feel depressed or discouraged, that is a sign that you need to talk to someone. You need to get help. Don't be too proud to ask for assistance or support at any time. You are a teacher, but you are also a human.

"I am only one, but still I am one. I cannot do everything, but still I can do something. I will not refuse to do the something I can do."

Helen Keller
1880-1968

Chapter Four

Be Careful How You Criticize

This chapter is absolute fiction based on real fact. Confused? Let me explain.

One of the greatest things a teacher can ever learn is *never to criticize a person, only criticize their actions.* This is a fundamental fact of effective teaching and it works in either your house or the schoolhouse. So I made up a story that sadly takes place in real life every day. You'll see what I mean.

Here is the story.

Mr. Browning is a classroom teacher. He doesn't officially have lunchroom duty but on this particular day, as he was walking through the cafeteria to the office, he noticed a young man purposely pull a chair out from a young lady as she was about to sit down. She fell on her behind and her lunch tray went flying. The young man started to laugh, until he saw Mr. Browning change directions and come toward the table. Mr. Browning went directly to the girl, who was more embarrassed than physically hurt. Another teacher also came over and Mr. Browning asked that teacher to assist the young lady. He then leaned over the young man, who we will call Steve, and began to "talk" to him in a rather elevated tone. He told Steve the following:

"I saw what you did and I can't believe that you are that stupid. Do you know you could have injured that girl permanently? I can't believe that you could be that uncaring and mean! There is no excuse for what you did! To add to your stupidity, you have the nerve to laugh! I plan to ask the principal to suspend you. You don't deserve to be here."

The more Mr. Browning talked, the more agitated he became. Mr. Browning knew not to touch Steve physically, but he didn't realize that he was, indeed, touching him emotionally.

Let's continue our hypothetical story about Steve.

Let's assume that Steve does get suspended for the rest of the day, and the next two days serves an in-school suspension. His dad is called and he is picked up and goes home shortly after lunch. His dad is very upset because he had to leave work to pick up his son. His dad adds additional punishment to Steve's sentence.

Steve has not had a good day, to say the least. That night, as Steve lies in bed, his thoughts might go something like this:

"Man, did I screw up today! I didn't mean to hurt her, or even make her fall. I've never seen Mr. Browning so mad. He was almost as mad as my dad gets. Mr. Browning called me stupid, just like my dad does. Mr. Browning said I was mean and uncaring. My mom calls me mean. What's the use? Maybe I am dumb. Maybe I shouldn't be around. Maybe they need to know what mean really is. Maybe I should show that Browning how much I hate him. Just maybe…"

Steve stops thinking about his day and his mind starts to work like the mind of a confused kid, a mind that's not fully developed, brain cells that don't make all the right connections because they haven't been fully connected. And, maybe, just maybe, adolescent things run through his head like revenge, suicide, destruction, and worse…

Does every kid react this way? No, thank goodness. Do some? You bet. You see, Mr. Browning attacked Steve, not his behavior. He didn't focus on what Steve did; he took away the value of who Steve is. Mr. Browning pulled the chair out from Steve's own self-esteem and may have done more damage to Steve than Steve did to the girl.

Let's give Mr. Browning another chance. Let's visualize the same scenario, but with a different response. This time Mr. Browning says the following:

"I saw what you did and I can't believe you would do something so stupid! Do you know you could have injured that girl permanently? Do you know why I am so upset? Because you are not stupid, you are bright. In fact, you are a very capable young man that I enjoyed having as a student, and I expect more from you. Steve, there is no excuse for what you did. Absolutely no excuse. I want you to think about that. And know that you are too smart to laugh at the embarrassment you caused that girl. I plan to ask the principal to suspend you because what you did just doesn't match who you are."

Steve gets exactly the same punishment in both cases. Dad acts exactly the same way, but that night, lying in bed, Steve will have different thoughts. Steve may think:

"Man, did I screw up today! I didn't mean to hurt her, or even make her fall. I've never seen Mr. Browning so mad. He was almost as mad as my dad gets. But Mr. Browning said I was bright. I didn't realize he enjoyed having me in class. Mr. Browning said he expected more from me. Man, I really messed up. I need to apologize to the girl and Mr. Browning."

Mr. Browning, in this scenario, not only disciplined the boy's behavior, he strengthened the boy's self-esteem. You see, by separating the behavior from the person, he can actually correct one while building the other.

I remember once when one of my own kids was caught fabricating an excuse for something they had done wrong. My wife and I focused more on their integrity and honesty than we did on the wrong they were guilty of. We talked about their long history of trustworthy behavior and how proud we were of them, but how this one incident conflicted with that expectation. We told them we loved them, respected them, and were disappointed in this behavioral choice. We hugged them and then took away the car keys and gave them a sentence of one month with no school activities or dates. We were honest, firm, and focused on their behavior, not on them as a faulty human being. We built them up while administering some tough discipline. It worked. It usually does.

Will all kids respond positively to this type of process? Of course they won't. But even if they throw a fit, consider you inhuman, or respond in what appears to be a negative way, you can rest assured that you have not added to their inventory of negative input. If you treat them as a worthy human being, no matter what the crime or punishment, you will be doing what is best.

Oh, by the way, this works in your house as well as the schoolhouse. Don't hurt the ones who love you by responding to their behavior with hurtful or critical messages. Every time your own child tests the appropriateness of their actions, be sure to let them know that you love them. Did you ever hear your mom or dad say to you, "If I didn't love you so much I wouldn't worry about where you are or what you are doing!" What a wonderful statement when you think about it.

When you criticize the behavior and not the human, you once more change lives.

◆ Always try to provide a positive environment for all students, remembering that students who are not self-motivated need more pep talks and more inspiration. You may even have to program positive comments at first. Eventually they will become part of your "life-changing" process.

◆ Every class, no matter what the subject, should stress vocabulary. Some students simply don't understand what some basic words mean. Stress comprehension of the words you use. Never assume that everyone understands everything. Don't ask a generic question like, "Does everyone understand what this word means?" You probably won't get the kid who doesn't understand to fess up. Instead, ask, "Who can explain what this word means?" Or use your name cards (see Cast of Characters chapter) to call on someone to explain a word.

◆ You can strengthen motivation by getting students off to a good start. Easier tests at the beginning of a semester may give someone with low confidence that extra boost they need for a quick, positive, reassuring start. Starting exams with a few "gimme" questions helps to give them a positive start and boosts confidence.

◆ Never, never, never criticize the student; only criticize their behavior. This is essential to becoming a teacher who makes a difference! How do you learn to do this? Revisit the situation in your own mind and ask yourself, "How could I have handled that in a more positive, effective manner?"

◆ Tell your students you love them no matter what their age or yours. You don't have to be corny or emotional, just honest. If you don't love them, why are you teaching?

◆ When kids are truly sad and need a hug, hug them. You won't get arrested if you display appropriate behavior. Use your head and do what is right. I wouldn't hug a high school girl because she was upset because her boyfriend broke up with her. I would hug her if she just found out her parents were in a car accident. If a third grader was crying because someone on the playground called her a name, and her dad would probably respond with a hug, I'd hug her. Common sense prevails. Think first, then act appropriately. Remember that all humans need to be loved.

◆ Never say "Shut up." Never. Not even to a dog. It just doesn't fit in the vocabulary of an educational professional. How would you respond if your principal told you to "Shut up!"

◆ Send positive notes about specific good behaviors to the student via writing, e-mail, post-it notes, or regular mail. Everyone loves to receive a supportive, positive communication. It helps reinforce good behavior and can change lives.

◆ If you administer punishment, make sure it is appropriate to the crime. If you aren't sure, ask a peer. And, it can't be said enough, be consistent in your discipline.

◆ Don't make a kid do push-ups, stand in the corner, push a pencil with his nose, or hold his breath—and never, ever hit a student as a form of punishment. Ask yourself how would you feel if your own child was subjected to this type of punishment.

◆ If you ask kids to write sentences as discipline, ask yourself why. Isn't there a better way to get the point across?

◆ Nobody needs a hug more than a kid who just returned from being chemically treated for lice. Do it in private and tell them you missed them. They need to know they aren't an outcast.

◆ Never embarrass a student in front of the class. It can draw battle lines. Who wants to be publicly embarrassed? Do you? If you think you may have done this, talk to the student after class, apologize for the comment, and refocus on their behavior.

◆ Never punish the whole class for what one student has done. You may question the whole class, but don't punish them all. What you would do if you were pulled over with a group of 20 cars on the expressway and given a ticket for speeding because the officer couldn't figure out which driver was the one on his radar screen?

◆ If you are really stuck trying to figure out who in the class was responsible for a specific act, sometimes you can get confidential help by calling a parent and seeing if you can find out via home connections. That helps solve some tough situations and keeps innocent kids out of the mess.

◆ Don't discipline by putting a student in the hall. Remember that kids in the hall are not being properly supervised. Being sent to the hall is public embarrassment. If you send a kid to the hall to take a test or exam, have them in a desk with a sign that reads, "Please be quiet. This student is taking a test." This tells the audience that it is not discipline, just an exam.

◆ Never engage in name-calling when disciplining students, or at any other time. It may come back to haunt you!

◆ When giving praise, be specific. Don't just say "good" or "super." That isn't specific enough. Tell them exactly why their paper or assignment was good. It takes a few seconds longer, but it is many times more meaningful.

◆ It is better to teach good behavior than to punish bad acts. Don't be afraid to teach kids manners. In fact, one teacher does a "Dear Abby" with her students when a manners question comes up. She will say to the kids, please write a "Dear

Abby" response to this question "Is it okay to chew gum with your mouth open?" Most of the time it reinforces the fact that the majority of the kids know the right answers.

Chapter Five

Trees and Kids

There is an unusual tree commonly known as the Chinese Bamboo Tree. It is real. Years ago I heard a speaker talk about it, using it to make a point. It stuck in my head. I even did some research to find out if the speaker was blowing smoke and made up the tree. He didn't.

The story goes like this. You prepare the soil, pick the right spot, then plant the Chinese Bamboo Tree. You water it and wait. But you wait an entire year and nothing appears. No bud, no twig, nothing. So you keep watering and protecting the area and taking care of the future plant, and you wait some more. You wait another year and nothing still happens. Okay, you are a persistent person not prone to giving up, so you keep on watering. You water, check the soil, start talking to the ground, maybe even click your heels in some kind of growing dance you read about in the *National Geographic*. Another year passes and still no sign of growth.

It has been three years. Should you give up? Someone told you that it might take a while to really see the fruits of your efforts, so you keep on keeping on. More water, more talk, more dancing. The neighbors are wondering. And another year passes. No tree.

You now make a decision. If there is no tree on this date one year from now you will stop watering. Period. So you begin year number five with the same passion as day number one. You water, you wait. You keep watering and keep waiting. You water some more and then, could it be? Is it really? Yep, there it is, something sticking out of the dirt. You come back the next day and WOW it has really grown! In fact you come back each day for about six weeks and finally the Chinese Bamboo tree stops growing—but it is over 80 feet tall! Yes, 80 feet in six weeks! Well, not really. It is 80 feet in five years.

The point is simple. If you had given up for even the shortest period of time, there would be no tree. It took almost impossible persistence. The Chinese Bamboo tree is there for one reason and one reason only—because you never gave up on it.

When I talk to teachers at workshops or institutes I find one who teaches first grade and I ask that person to mentally think of a student who they wouldn't mind see moving to another district. You get the drift, a student who is a real challenge. Let's give the student a name. I'll use my own name to be politically correct. The kid is named Jim. I ask the teacher if they ever had a student like Jim that they really worked hard with, tried every trick in the book, searched for new ways to meet the child's learning needs, and so on, but still felt that at the end of the year that Jim had not learned. That Jim was still a challenge, and although he met the minimum standards to pass, he was not on the teacher's list of proudest achievements. Most teachers usually agree that they have, or had, a Jim in their class.

Now we move to a second grade teacher and we pretend that they get Jim in the fall, work with him all year, watch their hair turn from brunette to shades of stressful gray, and by the end of the year feel they did their best, but it wasn't good enough.

Now, for a minute, let's talk about little Jimmy. He's not in special ed. Jimmy is just a jerk. Don't fall off your chair and gasp, "Did he call that kid a jerk?" I did, but not the jerk you are thinking of. My JERK is an acronym for Just Educationally Resistive Kid. He doesn't have ADD or any other alphabetized condition. He just doesn't like to learn and he resists it. He isn't a bad kid or a troublemaker. "Jimmys" exist in all sizes and shapes and even come in girl forms.

Let's jump to grade three. We have the same conversation all over again. Jim is passed on but he is a disappointment to every teacher so far, and they all worry that if things don't turn around Jim could become a troublemaker or an academic disgrace.

Jim holds his own in grade four. No big changes. He surely doesn't love school, but he isn't failing anything. He exhibits no passion for anything at the schoolhouse. And no signs of any real change either.

Grade five. Jim has a new teacher and all the other teachers try to warn her that Jim is, well, how do we say it? Jim is special, but not special ed. He exists, but barely. He will continue to be a challenge, but he's not a threat to safety. Jim is Jim. Try anything, but nothing will probably work. If you don't believe me, ask all of his previous teachers.

At semester break the new teacher makes a comment about Jim at a teachers meeting. With anticipated sadness, everyone listens. Here is what she says…

"Jim is quite a writer. He turned in a couple of stories and I told him he was very creative. He is now writing a mystery story and it is good! And he's also showing some talent in basketball. He's really growing too. I love his passion to play ball and write. He seems to thrive on the success of his hook shot and his imagination. I really enjoy that kid." Jim has arrived!

Was it the new teacher who pulled out Jim's hidden talents and secret love for learning? Was it some biological change that caused Jim to mature and become a better learner, a more serious student? Was it his physical abilities that expanded his self-esteem and made it easier for him to write?

Maybe it was a little of all these things, but it was also what I call the Chinese Bamboo Factor. Every teacher Jim had since he entered school worked hard providing opportunities for Jim to learn, to grow, and to become. Every teacher watered, fertilized, and cared for Jim. Even when the year ended and they were sometimes glad to pass him on to another teacher, they still knew that they had done *their best to give him the best*.

Oh, by the way, my story could stop and start at any grade. And Jim could be Janet, and the teacher could be a he rather than a she. It doesn't matter. What does matter is the Chinese Bamboo Factor—never, ever quit on a student. Even when you see no progress, it doesn't mean that the kid isn't processing something somehow somewhere.

One more thing, a big thing: the Chinese Bamboo Tree did start to grow very shortly after the seed was planted. The roots grew deep and strong for many years before there was any sign of a plant above ground. Sometimes that same thing happens with kids. They develop a foundation of learning. They learn to learn. They creep along doing the minimum, building their strengths (or finding them), and sometimes they just wait for the right combination of factors before they bloom. It may be the motivation of a certain teacher or a new found confidence or skill. It may be that all of a sudden "they get it" and learning becomes exciting. If we knew exactly what the formula was and how it worked for everyone, we could probably cure the ills of the world.

So what do we learn from the Chinese Bamboo Tree? I'd suggest the following:

- It takes patience to teach some, even most, kids.
- When you give up on a kid, you give up on a human being.
- Even when you don't see progress, if you do your best, it is probably happening.
- If something doesn't work with a kid, try something else—but never quit trying.
- Some of our best teaching doesn't "break soil" until all conditions are right.
- When you think you are growing a tree, you may be growing a root.
- Strong roots support strong trees.
- *Sometimes it takes a lot of patience to change a life.*

◆ If you sense they haven't learned the topic of the day, don't move on. If you are not sure, assess their learning before advancing. If they haven't mastered the topic, it may not be them, it may be the way you are teaching.

◆ Write a note or have a personal conference about behavior issues. Sometimes the written word has more impact. If you have a conference, ask "What can I do to help you?" If you write a note, always point out something good. It helps to mention how proud you are of the student when they do what is right.

◆ Remember that students have bad days too. One teacher, at the beginning of the year, tells her students to notify her at the start of the hour if they don't feel well or are just having a bad day. It won't happen as often as you think but it just may open a doorway for conversation and an opportunity to provide much needed assistance.

◆ Utilize peer tutors and peer counseling across grade level lines. Don't be afraid to cross the ill-fated building barriers (high school kids helping at the middle school, MS kids working with grade school students, etc.). Kids helping kids is almost always a win-win-win situation. The kids, at both levels, win. You certainly win.

◆ Always make an effort to challenge every ability level in every class. Make sure the low-motivated students are called on and challenged. It is best to tailor their questions to foster success. Make sure you give enough time to answer. And, of course, give each student an appropriate positive response. If you don't know, or remember, the correct way to ask questions and solicit responses, ask that a review of this important subject be conducted at a faculty meeting or in-service.

◆ Provide services for every student. Let them know they will participate in special programs. Here are some examples: Grades K-4: Self-Esteem Team, "Here's Looking at You," or PeaceBuilders; Grade 5: Dare; Grades 6-8: Teacher/Advisor Program; Grades 9+: LINK, Lifesavers, or SADD.

◆ Use your school's strengths, not weaknesses. If your school is small, involve as many as possible in co-curricular activities. Plays, for instance, should have 40 people in them instead of one; teams should have five scorekeepers, 15 cheerleaders, etc. If you can't offer 15 sports, then get as many involved in the four that you do offer.

◆ Have school-wide special events like spirit days, happy daze week, homecoming week, election week, environment week, etc. One school in our area celebrates the anniversary every year of when they went from being a junior high to a middle school. Classrooms can do the same thing with a week-long "special" topic.

◆ "Faith is the confident assurance that something we want is going to happen. It is the certainty that what we hope for is waiting for us, even though we cannot see it up ahead," Hebrews 11:6. Never lose faith in a student. Never lose your own faith.

◆ Of all the "R's" you teach, none is more important than responsibility.

"Talk does not cook rice."

Chinese proverb

Chapter Six

You Walk, They Follow

Not every teacher is the Pied Piper of excellence. It's sad but true. Still, I believe that most teachers are people who kids admire, look up to, want to emulate, and would follow anywhere.

Some of those teachers are truly unforgettable. Remember the Wicked Witch from the East in the chapter about Mr. Ruggles? She was unforgettable for the wrong reasons.

Dr. Ben, on the other hand, was on the side of the angels. He was one of the many, many educators who made those he met better people. I'll tell you why a little later.

There is a Native American saying, *"Do not judge any man until you have walked two moons in his moccasins."*

When I was just an upstart of a teaching administrator, I used to ride most of the bus routes at least once a year. It was kind of a moccasin thing. I didn't do it to check the distance of the trip or the expertise of the driver. I did it to know my kids better. I had a greater appreciation when I learned that a student rode the bus for 70 minutes every morning, after doing chores, and then put in a full day of school before riding another 50-60 minutes home. When I discovered that some of the kids were putting in longer hours than many of the district's employees, it helped me understand them a little better.

When I realized the size of their families and the economics of their living conditions, then saw their homes, farms, condos, apartments, or housing projects, it helped me fit into their moccasins a bit better. When I watched a Mom walk them to the bus, give them a kiss, and send them off surrounded by love and support, it made me understand them better. When no parents were to be seen, or no cars were left in the driveway because everyone had already left for work and two or three little kids meandered to the bus like orphans, it gave me an opportunity to understand those kids better.

I knew that I was only seeing a tiny segment of their lives, and the parents that left early to go to work may have been equally as loving and caring as those who walked their kids to the bus. But every bit of information allowed me to understand my kids better and thus do my job more effectively. I really encourage teachers to ride a school bus, visit your students' neighborhoods, or know the area where you work and they live.

On one of those long routes I learned a great deal from a veteran bus driver that I will call Ralph. One early morning, after the bus had wiggled its way along some snaky country roads, it pulled in front of a shack of a house. Two little kids wandered out with recycled lunch boxes and Wal-Mart bags that substituted for backpacks. The littlest, barely able to hike up the bus stairs, was a quiet little girl. She was a special needs kindergarten student. The older one was a first grade boy, slight in size, cute and clean. His name was Justin. When he got on the bus he scowled at Ralph and responded to Ralph's pleasant hello with a rather shocking retort, "I don't want to see my f__ing teacher and I don't want to go to that f__ing school either!"

Needless to say, as the young, idealistic educational leader of the school, I was ready to give the young lad a taste of appropriateness when I noticed Ralph's expression in the rearview mirror and he ever so slightly nodded "no" to me. So I sat back and listened.

Ralph quietly said, "Now, Justin, you just find your seat and think about what you just said."

Ralph kept driving and I kept quiet, and once in a while I thought I heard the "f" word from little Justin who was just two rows behind me and engaged in conversation with his buddies.

When we got to school, the kids quickly marched off the bus. When Justin passed Ralph, Ralph gently told him to wait outside the bus doors for him. After all the kids were off the bus, and before Ralph walked to the back to check seats and windows, he called Justin to come back on the bus. Justin got back on. His eyes were wet. Ralph put his arm around Justin and this little kid looked up at him and said, "I'm sorry. I'm trying not to say it. It's just so hard to remember."

Ralph replied, "I know, but you have to work at it harder. It just isn't right to use that word anywhere. I'm proud of you for trying. Maybe tomorrow we can get to school and home and you will not say it once all day. What do you think?" Justin smiled and with a slight pat on the back from Ralph went off to class.

Ralph turned to me and asked, "Jim, have you met his folks?"

I wasn't sure if I had. Ralph told me that they are unable to say one sentence without using the "f" word. Not a sentence. And it goes for both his mom and dad, or mom and step-dad, or whatever.

Ralph continued, "Not bad folks, but they just don't get it. I've been working with Justin and we are making progress."

I learned as much on that bus ride as I did in several of my educational administration graduate classes. Ralph was not just a driver, he was also a teacher. Ralph had taken the time to walk a few steps in Justin's shoes and by knowing the circumstances he was able to adjust Justin's behavior. It was reassuring to me that Justin was lucky to have this wise old man as a mentor. And then I realized, I was just as lucky.

I wonder how most of us would have handled Justin's language if we didn't know about his home? What would we do if we hadn't walked even one moon in his tattered old Nike look-alikes?

Even when we think we know our kids, we might not.

I remember when she came to my office and asked to speak with me.

She started the conversation by saying, "Remember during our LTS (Love, Trust, Success) Class when you said if we ever had a problem we could come to you?"

I kidded with her that indeed I remembered saying that but I was just joking. She smiled, and then she asked if we could close the door. Normally I leave it open an inch or two, but instinct and her expression told me to close it.

"I'm pregnant," she said. Her eyes quickly filled with tears. "I have no one to turn to for help. Will you help me?"

I wanted to get out of my seat and go and give her a hug, but in one of those legal workshops the school sends us to I remember being told that the hug police would toss me into the fires of hell if I even thought of hugging a girl over the age of nine. So I sat there and said three of the dumbest things I could ever say.

"This isn't the end of the world."
"Have you told your mom or dad?"
"Does the father know?"

Here's a shocker for you. I have never been pregnant, nor have I been in the situation of being personally involved with a pregnancy before marriage. So what do I know about this being the end of the world for a sixteen-year-old girl? I knew nothing. My comment was insensitive at best, but certainly thoughtless to the fullest degree. I'm surprised she didn't get up and walk out. Who needs help from an imbecile?

My next statement was even worse. She responded to it by reminding me that she didn't know her mom and couldn't remember her. She informed me that her dad was a drunk, and a mean one. She then told me that her dad had threatened both her and her sister that if they ever got pregnant, he would kill them. I followed those comments by asking her if he had ever hurt them physically. She said no but that she feared him when he was drunk. She was obviously afraid of him. I believed her.

And then she said she didn't know who the father was.

Dumb, dumb, dumb. Instead of listening to my own lectures, I proceeded to walk out on a limb that could have broken with each step. You see, I judged her before I walked with her.

I saw an honor student, involved with school activities, well liked, polite, and well groomed. What I was about to learn was she was a frequent drinker, sexually active, and had given permission for more than one boy to have a relationship with her one night when she was at a party, intoxicated, and subsequently passed out. When she woke up she was in the house trailer of a friend, had been molested, and now she was pregnant.

You have probably heard of the movie *Dumb and Dumber*. My next statement to her could be titled "Dumbest Ever." I asked her if she called the police after the party. She looked at me as if I was subhuman and then asked me what was she supposed to say to the police?

Sarcastically she said, "Excuse me, Mr. Officer, I went to this underage party, got drunk, told a couple of guys who wanted to have sex with me to go ahead if they ever got the chance, then passed out, and they took me up on the offer."

"No," she continued, "I went home and cried a lot and thought about my life, your class, and the mess I might be in. And now I *am* in it. And I don't have anyone on the face of this earth I can go to except you. Can you help?"

In spite of my stupidity she still wanted my help. I sat back, embarrassed at how I had handled this, but more embarrassed because I thought I had walked in her moccasins, I thought I knew this girl, but I really didn't. I didn't even remember that she lived with only her dad, and although I knew he was a heavy drinker, I never put two and two together.

By the way, I put her in contact with a woman who specialized in pregnancy issues for young girls through a government agency. They met the very next day and started counseling. About ten days later the girl came into my office again and asked, like before, if she could close the door. She said the lady was wonderful, that her life was on a different track, that she planned to tell her dad (with help from the lady) during the coming weekend, but things had suddenly changed. She miscarried the night before. And then she cried once again. This time I forgot about those nasty hug police and I hugged her. This time I had walked a few steps in those moccasins and I was a much better listener and teacher.

Today she is a happily married wife with high school kids of her own. And those kids are loved.

No one told me that when I taught a class to high school sophomores, they would be asking me to help with such important issues. No one taught me at the university how to get to know my students, and how important it was. No one prepared me for the fact that indeed, in many ways I would never expect, I would be changing lives.

Then there was Dr. Ben. He was the freshman Dean of Students at my high school. I remember meeting him for the mandatory 15-minute "get-to-know-the-student" session at the beginning of the year. This "one-on-one" meeting was designed to review your master class schedule and begin the process of working with each student as they developed their four-year sequence of classes. We called it "suits meet students" time. My "suit" was good old Dr. Ben. He was a neat looking guy and very friendly. He asked me a bunch of questions none of which I remembered by dismissal of the same day. What I did remember was that he gave me a card with the time of my second appointment on it.

Visualize, if you will, a skinny, pimple-faced thirteen-year-old with black horn rimmed glasses, brown eyes, and probably wearing a smirk on his face. That was me. I was innocent and only a blip in a school of over 4,000 kids. I was outgoing, had friends, liked sports, had a paper route, and even had a girl I was infatuated with who I watched from a distance while she won the hearts of upper classmen.

My second appointment with Dr. Ben was a little longer. We didn't talk much about classes, more about me, what I liked, my brothers and sister, and he even pumped me a little about my parents. I guess at that meeting I reluctantly told him my parents were separated. He gave me another card at the end of that meeting for the next week.

We met a bunch of times. I thought it was what every freshman did until one of my friends told me he only had one meeting with his dean. I discovered I was the only one who had won the lottery on dean meetings.

After a while, Dr. Ben had me sharing a lot with him. He knew that my parents both had drinking problems. He learned that there was another man involved with my mom. That I was basically the male of the house because my brothers were eight years older, had left after high school, and didn't come home very often. He knew I had felt a lot of responsibility for a sister eight years younger. In fact, Dr. Ben got me to tell him more than I told anyone, including any family member or friend. And then he taught me some important skills.

He taught me how to cope and how to channel my anger. He made me understand that drinking was an illness and that intoxicated people did and said things they didn't always mean. He made me understand that I could become a better person by learning what works and doesn't work in life. He also taught me that I wasn't alone with my struggles. There were lots of kids and lots of families like mine. He gave me strength and courage.

I remember one day lying in bed listening to a violent argument, including some hurtful language, and knowing my little sister was listening to all of this as well, and I forgave my parents and knew, at that moment, that when I had children of my own they would not go through this. It was Dr. Ben that taught me how to process these thoughts, open my heart, and, as trite as it sounds, to make lemonade out of lemons. And he did it because he sensed, during our 15-minute mandatory meeting, that my moccasins walked through some rough terrain, and he took the time to walk there with me.

The little boy who learned the wrong words at home, the girl who showed me that what you see is not always what you get, and the skinny little 13-year-old who didn't want anyone to know about his family were all lucky to have experiences with educators who changed their lives. Experiences that were the result of educators who took the time to get to know their students before they judged them.

A good teacher walks the talk. A good teacher is an example of good behavior. He or she is a good role model.

Teachers might not have all the answers, but the good ones at least will try to live what they preach.

I had little respect for the coach who swore at us in the locker room and then disciplined us for swearing on the playing field. I had little respect for the overweight physical education teacher. I wasn't impressed by the teacher who used sarcasm with some kids but honey with others. It was obvious to me as a student which teachers wanted to make a difference and which were there just to get a paycheck. Kids aren't stupid. They can see through our transparent facades. They know when we don't walk the talk but just talk to talk. They know when we don't have a clue about them, and when some really don't care about them at all. And, in spite of all this, some of these less-than-stellar teachers *can* get kids to learn, but many can't. And, unfortunately, some even hurt kids in the process.

There is an old American proverb that says, *"You are judged by what you do, not by what you say you will do."* There is another saying that says, *"Words to live by are just words unless you live them. You have to walk the talk to make a difference."*

As teachers, we have the opportunity to transform lives. We can inspire children to become worthwhile citizens, caring parents, and fine people. We can do it through educating them with fact and content. We can do it by training them to think and process. And we can do it by knowing who they are and loving them no matter what. We can't forget that when we walk, they follow. And if we know who they are, we can walk with them better.

P.S. Remember that girl I talked about who I watched break others' hearts from afar when I was a freshman? I married her. Dr. Ben also taught me about patience.

◆ When Andrew comes to school discouraged or down, ask him why. Take a moment and tell him that you notice something is different, then compassionately try to find out what. Kids may tell you things they wouldn't tell others. That single question might change their life.

◆ Kids know when you care. They also know when you don't. Kids aren't stupid.

◆ Attend school events. I know you are busy, but everyone is. It makes a HUGE difference when you are involved and you can say to kids that you were there, that you were proud of them, and that you enjoyed watching them.

◆ A simple note congratulating a student on winning an award or playing in a game, and if appropriate, mentioning that you saw them do it, means a lot.

◆ Let your students know that you care about them, and do it in no uncertain terms. Be open with them. Touch them emotionally. Show them you care about them as a person. Welcome them back after an absence. Congratulate them for a good answer or score. Comment on a positive action. Mention that they look nice. Thank them for doing a good job or demonstrating a positive behavior.

◆ Treat students the way you want to be treated—with respect, dignity, and compassion. Do this always, not just once in a while.

◆ Never be buddies with students. Maintain a professional relationship. But don't be unfriendly. You can be friends and still remain a caring, loving adult.

◆ If you personally know a student through family, church, or outside activities, and they call you by your first name or a nickname outside of school, talk to them about calling you by your more formal name inside school. Do this before an uncomfortable situation develops. They will understand what is right.

◆ When a student has his or her mom or dad as their teacher or administrator, or sees them in the same building, they should feel comfortable calling them Mom or Dad. Everyone knows the relationship and it is strange to call your parents Mr. or Mrs. If you are ever in this situation, talk to your kids and find a comfort zone that works for them.

"The best way to destroy an enemy is to make him your friend."

Abraham Lincoln
1809-1865

Chapter Seven

The Wisdom of Mr. B

He may have been the best teacher I had for demonstrating effective teacher strategies. He was also a bit odd, in a very positive way.

Lots of kids wanted to be in his class, but not me. He taught English. Until my senior year in high school, English was my least favorite class. In fact, I loathed English. My spelling and grammar were below par, my writing talents were non-existent, and I had never read a book that wasn't assigned, expected, or forced. I had not learned to appreciate reading novels or plays, and I didn't like anything that rhymed. I loved math and science and tolerated social studies, but I did not like English.

My parents, well actually my mom, had her own interpretation of grades in our house. A "B" meant you could probably do better. A "C" meant curfew. A "D" meant death. We never asked what an "F" meant. I think we knew. Anyway, we were all expected to do well. If we got a "B," it was acceptable but it usually prompted lecture #53, the substance of which was "How to Reach Your Potential." So, in spite of my internal problems with English, I knew that I had to at least manipulate a "B" out of the teacher in order to survive at home. I did it, but it took some work.

It was even harder during one year with Mrs. Breckenridge, who smelled like the perfume-testing counter at Macy's, died her long hair blonde, strutted instead of walked, and was at least 120 years old, or so it seemed. She set teaching back 200 years.

Teachers Change Lives 24/7

If there ever was a teacher more boring, I'd like to meet her. Not. She loved to give essay tests and liked the neat, polite, and friendly boys best. I was very neat, very polite, and very friendly that year. I got a "B" each quarter. I don't remember learning a thing. You'll learn more about her later in this book.

When my senior year came around everyone was saying things like, "Try to get Mr. B," "He's fun, interesting, and a bit goofy, but you learn a lot," "He will get you ready for college," "He's a great English teacher," and "He makes English interesting."

No matter what, I could have cared less. I wasn't worried about college English. I told myself that my grades were fine, my ACT acceptable, and that I'd make it fine. I didn't need Mr. B. or his "inspiration."

When I got my schedule I discovered that I had Mr. B for English IV. Big deal. No cartwheels by this kid.

On the first day of class I knew this guy was different. For one thing, he looked different. He was short, stocky, wore glasses, was balding, but kept a few long strands of hair that he could flip over his dome to delay the inevitable. I remember seeing him at a track meet once and the wind was blowing and the long hairs were standing straight up. It looked like hair antennas.

He wore pink shirts and had a pink tie. He drove a pink Mustang. He had two daughters and one was deaf. He told us about her every so often. He looked like a strong, tough little guy. Almost like a gangster with his dark hair, thick eyebrows, and a stare that sank you into submission. He had a funny voice, not high, not low, just kind of funny. He dressed like a professional every day. He laughed a lot, with half cackle, half belly laugh. I liked him immediately.

He taught college level English, English IV for the regular kids, and English M. They tried to hide the fact that English M was for kids with learning challenges. We affectionately called it English for Mutants. Kids are cruel. (I guess that includes me.)

I also learned a lot from watching him teach. He never sat at his desk when he was teaching. I can't even tell you where his desk was because all I remember is that he walked non-stop except when he was using the boards. He must have known the research about proximity that says that a student hears and learns more when the teacher is close, or when the teacher roams in an unpredictable pattern. You never knew where he would end up so you were always watching and listening.

I also witnessed an expert teacher who could teach in more than one or two ways. And a teacher who meant it when he said there wasn't a stupid question. He encouraged us to ask as many questions as possible if we had any doubt about what he was teaching. He meant it. If you weren't the sharpest tack on the board he wouldn't get frustrated if you asked him the same question more than once. I think it was a challenge for him to find ways to provide an answer you understood.

I remember a kid named Bruce who said to me once when Mr. B was teaching us some grammar rule, "I don't get it." I turned and said to Bruce, "Ask him to explain it again." Bruce replied, "He already explained it three times."

Mr. B heard us talking and asked what was going on. I told him I didn't quite understand what he was explaining. He smiled and gave his normal response, "Well, let me try to approach this from another angle." And he did, and it was almost magical how he could create so many new and different teaching examples. When he was done he said, "And now, Mr. Burgett, do you and your neighbor understand?"

Oh, that reminds me. He almost always called us Mr. or Miss. He very seldom used our first names, unless he was making a reference to us. It was kind of neat.

He gave lots of assessments. Some were simple one- or two-question quizzes. Sometimes he would have us write a paragraph incorporating what we had been taught. Sometimes we exchanged papers and we had to grade them on our own. He would collect them and if both students missed the point of the lesson he would talk to us the next day, or write long notes, or do anything to make sure we had a chance to learn it properly. He was very concerned that we learned today's lesson before moving on.

In the upper left hand corner of the front chalkboard was a box that contained our assignments. Five days were always listed. However, if we were learning, and it took longer or shorter than he had planned to move forward, he made no apologies if he changed the assignments. His mantra was always the same. You are here to learn. That is our job. He often told us that he got paid for his job with money and we get paid for ours through the opportunity for a better life. He would say, "I can't make you learn, but I can, and will, do my best to give you every chance." He said that often and we knew he meant it.

Grammar can be boring, even if you are a great teacher. Mr. B hated anything that was boring. I remember once when he could see our interest fading, he stopped teaching, moved to the center of the room, and asked a question.

"Do you know how to sell a duck to a deaf person?" He asked.

No one responded. They had no idea what he was talking about. Maybe he was going to talk about his daughter. Maybe he was introducing a new topic. Maybe he was having an aneurism. No one had a clue.

He asked the question a few more times, always pausing to wait for an answer. Finally he took a step forward, put his hands to his mouth, and shouted, "Do you want to buy a duck?"

Everyone roared. And then, without another word, he returned to teaching. He had awakened us, brought us back, and, as always, made class interesting. He made learning enjoyable. He was a master at teaching.

Mr. B asked lots of questions. He never let you off the hook when he asked you a question. He would wait several seconds for a response. If you didn't know the answer, he would tease you with another chance. Sometimes he would make the question multiple choice or true and false. Sometimes he would reword it. Sometimes he would have you pick two people who could give you a hint, but not the real answer. He made a little game out of it. If you finally came up with the right answer, he might applaud or he might have the whole class give you a cheer. No matter what, when he was done with you two things had happened. First, you ended up giving the right answer, and second, you felt better. Yes, you felt better. He never made you feel silly or stupid. He never put anyone down, even if he was correcting a behavior or asking you to pay attention, or questioning your work ethic. He treated everyone with dignity and class. I think those are the two words that defined his teaching as well. Dignified and classy.

We read out loud most weeks from the novel we were assigned. He would hand out a sheet with words or punctuation marks on it, by seat number. It was kind of a game. Everyone read until they came to the pre-designated word or punctuation mark, and then the next person took over. Picture it if you will. The first person in the row read until they came to a word on the list in front of them. When they read that word they stopped. The person behind them started up immediately and this went from the front person to the back person in the row, and then Mr. B took a turn as the extra person in the row. When he was done the first person in the next row started. The game was such that you read a paragraph or two and often stopped mid-sentence. The next person had to keep up the timing and appropriate intonation of their voice.

He took this seriously and it was not only fun, but was kind of cool. When Mr. B read, he read with the kind of passion that made the story come alive, and he inspired us to do the same. If a student was absent, he randomly picked kids to be placeholders for the missing students and they had to fill their spots as well as their own. The game was to read in a seamless manner from person to person. Once in a while he would stop and we would discuss what we read. The books became real, and enjoyable. We mixed a little theater with reading.

I remember once when a student wasn't reading with enough volume or force. He asked the kid to stand up and read with gusto. He stood up but not much changed. He then had the kid stand on his desk and read with real gusto. It was a funny way to get the student to project his voice, but it worked.

We would read books, interpret them, talk about them, make them come alive, and debate them. I can never remember him mocking or discouraging any of our personal interpretations of books. In fact, he would rub his chin, cackle a bit, and say "interesting." He looked like Jack Nicholson when he did that. He encouraged you to think and to share your thoughts.

By the way, Mr. B made reading fun, and because of him I became an avid reader.

I still have an essay that I wrote in English IV. I kept it because it was the first essay that I ever wrote that wasn't magical. Let me explain. I wrote my essays in blue. When they came back they were red! It was pure magic. Or maybe it was all the correction marks and comments. Essay writing wasn't my forte.

One time, early in my senior year, I wrote an essay about religion. When I turned it in, it was blue. When it came back, it was still blue! In fact, the only red on it was the grade and a short comment. The grade was not an "A" but an "A+" The comment read, "Mr. Burgett, your writing was so interesting I forgot to search for your many and frequent grammar and spelling errors. Keep up the good work." He then told me privately that he was looking forward to my next paper, and he hoped the grammar and spelling would be as good as the content.

It was obvious that he had given me a "bye" on the grammar and spelling and at the same time had set higher expectations for future work.

From that point on I had all my papers proofed and checked before submission. And when I say all, I mean in every class, at every grade, from then until today. I used my trusty spell checker (my tattered hand-me-down *Webster's Dictionary*), and I made sure that I turned in as good a paper as I could. I earned an "A" from Mr. B each quarter. But more important than that, for the first time in my life, I enjoyed English.

I learned a number of things from Mr. B. One was how to begin a class. Even though he taught high school, I used his technique for kids in grade school, middle school, and high school, and still use it for seminars and workshops when applicable.

Mr. B started the class in the doorway. He did this almost every day. He greeted every student as they came in. Sometimes it was a handshake or a pat on the back, sometimes just a friendly hello, sometimes he spoke to you individually, but he always made you feel welcome. He might say something like, "My, someone smells great!" or "Wait until you see what you got on your test!" (You never knew where that one was going!). He might say, "I saw you play ball last night," or "Good to see you again, Mr. Burgett." He had a plethora of greetings but you had a feeling they were all real and all from the heart. *He made you feel welcome. Every day.*

Mr. B didn't have many students who were tardy. He seldom started class until the last student was coming in, even if it was a second past the bell. He was not anal retentive about everyone being in their seat with 100% buttock contact when the bell chimed, like some other teachers who probably needed a bit more zest in their lives.

Mr. B would follow the last student in and his first utterance to the class was always something like, "Good to see you." Or he would say, "I have been excited about what we are going to learn today for weeks." *It was always positive.* And then he started teaching. He frequently told us that he had "bell to bell" to make you all geniuses, so we couldn't waste any time. And he would teach bell to bell. Even tests, group work, and individual study time was given importance in the learning process. But the real key to his magic was that he made you *want* to use class time wisely. *He made you want to learn.*

He greeted each student. He started each class on time. He taught bell to bell. He was organized but flexible. He made teaching fun, but meaningful. He made reading enjoyable, but challenging. He tested our abilities, creativity, and our insight. He never made anyone feel silly or stupid. And when things didn't fit his mold, he changed the mold.

If a student came in late and said they forgot a book, had to go to the bathroom, stayed too long talking to their last teacher, etc., he responded with a smile and said something like "Life is good" and invited them in. He didn't say it was okay, or send them to the tardy police; he just put it in perspective and moved on. If a student was late a couple of times, he disappeared in the hall with that student before they entered the room. He probably was reminding the kid how valuable his "bell to bell" time was and that coming in late took precious minutes away from everyone. He would ask the kid to respect him and the others by trying hard to be on time. And guess what? When treated with respect, you respond with respect. The kid wasn't late again.

The greatest lesson in teaching came one winter day when a good friend of mine, one of the varsity basketball players, was blessed by Mr. B's wisdom. It happened at the beginning of the class. The boy's name was Eric. He was an early arriver to class and Mr. B had pulled him inside the classroom for a conversation. He happened to be talking to him near the corner of the room, close to where I sat. I heard the conversation. It went something like this….

"Eric, I saw last night's game. I brought my wife and daughters. I wanted them to see you. The team did quite well. I'd say we have a championship in our future."

"Thanks, Mr. B. We have one of the best teams in years and we should win conference and could even win the Sectionals," Eric responded.

Mr. B continued, "Eric, I noticed that you didn't play again last night. I've seen a few games this year, but I haven't seen you play yet. I told my family you might not get in. You have said we have a great team, but how do you rate our coach?"

Eric said, "We have a super coach. He really knows how to get us to win!"

"Well, I agree! He seems to know what he is doing. I guess that is why he has you on the bench and the team is winning left and right," Mr. B said.

I was a little shocked and thought his comments just didn't come out right, but then Mr. B continued by saying, "I guess if the team is winning they really don't need you to play, but I'm proud of you and that is why I brought my family to the game."

Needless to say, Eric was a bit confused, even ruffled. He looked (down) at Mr. B and said, "You know *I want* to play, and sometimes I get a little discouraged sitting on the bench."

"Discouraged!" Mr. B almost yelled, and then continued, "Why, Eric, you don't get it, do you? We are winning *because* you are on the bench!"

And now Eric was angered. He was basically a quiet kid but he raised his voice a little and came right back at Mr. B and said, "I don't know what you are trying to do, hurt my feelings or just make a statement?"

And then the wisdom of Mr. B emerged. I can't possibly quote him word for word because he was far more eloquent than I could ever be, but basically he told Eric that indeed Eric didn't understand. He reminded Eric that he had agreed they had an outstanding team with an exceptional coach. And then Mr. B said that the only reason our team could beat everyone around the area was because every night they practiced against highly talented players and they were ready for any competition. Eric replied that the team did not play every night, but Mr. B quickly corrected him by saying that indeed they did. He reminded Eric that at practice the team scrimmaged and played against each other.

Mr. B asked if the starters often played the second- string team, and Eric replied that of course they did. Mr. B thanked Eric for confirming his point. The point being that the only way the starters could be so successful was because they played against equal, if not better, competition on a regular basis, and that competition included Eric. Mr. B continued by telling Eric that the coach recognized his talent and his ability and had him on the team for that reason. Sure, he wasn't a starter, but he was just as important to the success of the team as anyone else, and that was why he brought his family, why he was so proud of Eric, and why Eric meant so much to the school. And he concluded by reaching up and giving Eric's neck a little squeeze and telling Eric to keep up the good work.

You see, Eric had been very discouraged about not playing. Eric's mother had called Mr. B about it, fearing that Eric might even quit. She and Eric's father didn't know what to do but knew how much Eric respected Mr. B. Mr. B took over from there. In one very brief exchange he made Eric go from being discouraged to encouraged, from thoughts of quitting, to being motivated to work even harder. I swear that Eric left that classroom taller than when he entered it. Mr. B was, quite simply, amazing.

Over the years I met a few students who failed Mr. B's class. They failed to take advantage of his unique teaching style, his ability to question, present, assess, motivate, and to squeeze every bit of ability out of you. They failed to respond to his way of keeping you involved, to his caring attitude, and to the positive teaching environment he fostered. They failed to accept his skill at moving you in the right direction. They failed his class, but he never failed anyone. Nor did he give up on anyone.

And that is the wisdom, and wonder, of Mr. B. A master at changing lives.

◆ Start the class with a warm welcome. Greet students as human beings. Do this as often as possible. Maybe greet them with a handshake, maybe a pat on the back, maybe a general comment about how good it is to see them, maybe a word about a new hairdo, or a nice shirt, or someone that smells good. No matter how you do it, do it often, and do it from the heart.

◆ Communicate individually and independently. One teacher uses the Carol Burnett "ear tug" to tell a student every time she sees him using inappropriate behavior. No one knows what is going on except the teacher and student.

◆ Have inspirational speakers fire up your students. If you are unsure how good the speaker may be, invite them to speak during the last 15 minutes of the period or 15 minutes before art, etc. That way they have less to prepare for, are not so intimidated, aren't on the spot for a long time if they are poor speakers, and you don't face the embarrassment if kids don't have any questions for them or if kids lose interest. If they are really good presenters, you can ask them back for a longer time. All kids like guest speakers if they are interesting, and everyone can survive 15 minutes if the speaker is a dud.

◆ Tell your class stories about people who have overcome failure, or about people who have become successful. Tell these stories often. Kids love stories and they can be exceptionally motivating. Try to make the story fit the curriculum or current events.

◆ Touch your students appropriately. There is nothing wrong with a handshake, a pat on the back, or an appropriate hug. Use your head and common sense and let kids know you care.

◆ Tell students when you're having a bad day or don't feel well. They'll usually cooperate. It's amazing.

◆ Remember who you aren't. You aren't the nurse so don't fix things that should be handled by her. You aren't the psychologist so refer things that are beyond your ability to fix to these trained professionals. You aren't the administrator so check when you consider a decision that might be covered by school policy or past practices and you aren't sure what your parameters are. You get the picture.

◆ Mark your calendar when someone experiences a crisis. If the teacher down the hall loses a husband, or a mother, or someone in your building faces a serious situation, be sure to send a card, be there for them, offer to help, etc. But mark your calendar one year ahead, and then, on the one-year anniversary, simply give them a card that says you are thinking about them, praying for them, or holding them in your heart. It will be one of the most thoughtful things that happen to them on that day.

"The only thing of value we can give kids is what *we are*, not what *we have*."

Leo Buscaglia
1924-1998

Chapter Eight

The Secret of PILY

The Xerox repairman is a really nice guy, and I'm fairly sure he thinks the same of me after our experience with Harold, but you really need to hear the *rest of the story...*

This experience takes place when I held the honor (?) of being a high school principal, district superintendent, and taught a high school class—at the same time. I was a busy boy, to say the least. I was also obviously in a very small district.

Earlier in the day, Harold, the Xerox copier, went on strike. (Yes, we named all of our machines. We considered them partners in the educational process.) Harold was mammoth in size and the only copier in the district. I called the "800" repair number and probably spoke to someone in Peru, India, or Georgia. I reported that Harold had an internal problem demonstrated by the fact that he was spitting up papers that bore only faint facsimiles to legible print. We finally came to an agreement on terms and I begged that she send a repairman ASAP since a school without a copier is like a car without an engine, a baby without a mother, a fishing pole without a hook—you get the point. I even mentioned that I might need to shut down the entire district if they couldn't send emergency help. She was most helpful and promised a serviceman that very day. By the end of our conversation she too had empathy for Harold.

A few hours later a serviceman called and said he could be there about 4:30 p.m., and asked if that would work. I told him we closed at 4:30 but I would be there to let him in and would stay until the job was completed. His best guess was that Harold needed a new drum. I had no clue what he meant but tried to sound like it was a serious internal disorder. Poor Harold.

At 4:45 the white truck pulled up. All the employees had left the auditorium and I was the only person around. I greeted the repairman, who was named Jerry, and directed him to Harold's room. A quick assessment told him that Harold indeed needed a new drum. He had one with him but it would take at least 90 minutes to replace so he would come back in the morning. I begged him to reconsider and asked him if the job could be done quicker if he had help. He agreed it wouldn't take as long, but help was not on the way. I offered my limited services. He said it was against Xerox policy. I faked a quick look around and told him I wouldn't tell anyone if he didn't. He laughed, I rolled up my sleeves, took off my tie, and we got to work.

Within a few minutes, and with cold Pepsis to drink, we were working like a well-oiled team. I retrieved parts from the truck, held the light, vacuumed where and when told, and was what might be called a third arm or "go-fer." Before you knew it, Harold was humming again and spitting out dark black copies like a muscled 21-year old (human, not copier).

Jerry and I bonded during the hour we spent together. When he left the building and got into his truck I'm sure he was thinking that I was a nice guy, fun to work with, and probably fun at school. I thought the same of him. And even though we only knew each other's first names and nothing much more about each other, we were genuinely kind and caring during our hour of repair work.

It was almost six o'clock when I left the office and headed home. It was only a five-minute drive. I parked in the garage and entered the house. My wife and youngest son were in the kitchen. My son, who was maybe six or seven at the time, asked if we could play catch, or do something. I responded quickly by saying to him, "Can't you wait until I change my clothes before you schedule my time?" It was totally inappropriate. My wife reminded me that we had a church meeting that night. I looked at her with an expression that wouldn't earn me many points from the Big Guy himself. So when I walked to the bedroom, I felt terrible. I went into my office—you know, the one with the porcelain seat—and sat there with nothing biological to do except ponder. I thought about my son's brown eyes and the disappointment he displayed when I snapped at him. I thought about the look my wife gave me, a look that said "typical response from Jim." And then, for some reason, I thought about the Xerox repairman who, only minutes before, had almost become my best friend. I had treated him better than I had treated my own family.

There are some key facts we need to consider at this point. First, my family loves me and I love them. My wife chose me, and God knows she could have done better. My kids didn't have a choice, but over the years we have all kind of grown fond of each other—I think they call it love. Here are people who want me to spend time with them, love them, and be part of their lives. I can't say any of this applies to the Xerox repairman, as nice as he was and as good a company as Xerox is. Yet, in perspective, it was the repairman of a paper copier that I treated better than my own family.

The main point here is that I should be able to treat everyone, at school, at home, and in between, with dignity and respect, and I shouldn't run out of love for the ones that mean the most to me, my own family, ever. No excuses allowed.

So, after several minutes of coming to grips with a problem that had been festering for a long time, I had a small brainstorm. I went to my real office (where the chair is upholstered) and got out a sticky label. I took a marker and wrote on it PILY. I then went to the garage door, and on the trim of the door, in the garage, I stuck the label about head high. And then I went into the kitchen, told my son we had a few minutes to play before dinner, and apologized to my wife. I also told her that I would be doing better when I got home from work in the future. She simply looked at me and said, "We'll see." That, too, was a reality check.

The next night when I came home I pulled in the garage and started to walk into the house. Things were pretty much the same. I was Mr. Nice Guy at work and most of my energy was spent before I reached my house. But this time, before I walked into the house, I was greeted by an eye-level sign that spelled "PILY," and it made me think. It also made me stop and take a second to rhetorically dump my problems and stress in the garage and not take them inside with me.

PILY? People Inside Love You.

The Xerox repairman deserves to be treated with respect. Making him laugh, brightening his day, giving him a reason to enjoy what he does are all worthy goals. Still, nothing is more important than remembering that there are others who depend on you for a lot more. They love you and they want you to love them back. The people in your house outscore the people at the schoolhouse.

Teaching is a stressful job. Kids consume our energies and sometimes our emotions. Their situations can break our hearts and cause discouragement. Their behavior can cause us angst and consternation. Their needs can drain our energy and our outlook. While all of this is true, we can never let the job infringe on our own personal relationships.

Forgive what might be considered a sexist statement, but I often think of the women who not only teach but also are wives and moms and daughters themselves. They frequently take care of the house, and the schedule, and work full time. They balance a lot more than most men I know. Not always, and not in every situation, but often. Most are spectacular. They care for their own kids and dozens of others, and they usually come home to a family that needs a dinner, clothes that need washing, lunches that need to be made, and homework that needs assistance. And they get it done. Of course, at times they too run out of energy and patience. It is then when the people inside need to remember that working and parenting, or working and partnering, or working and just living, take special skills, effort, and support.

The Secret of PILY is never to forget that we all need to work together—at school, at home, and in between. And that *People Who Love You* will love you even more if you save some energy, patience, and passion just for them.

It all fits in with maintaining the balance between your house and the schoolhouse, and it is a very important component of being an outstanding teacher and person. If you are to make a difference 24/7, you must work on it 24/7.

The secret of PILY can help.

◆ If you have had a bad day at school, dump it in the garage before you walk into your house after work. Then, when you have a few quiet minutes, think about why your day was bad and see if you can do something to make tomorrow better.

◆ Ask those you live with about their day. Focus the interest and discussion on everyone, not just on you.

◆ Help with homework, with the dishes, folding the laundry, putting the cars away, and/or taking out the garbage. If another member of the family normally performs this task, your help will not only brighten their day, but it can make relationships stronger.

◆ Studies have shown that life expectancy increases if you kiss your spouse good-bye or hello every day. If you don't do this now, why not begin this practice? If needed, warn your spouse so your new behaviors don't result in a premature heart attack!

◆ Send your kids off to school and greet them in the evening in a calm, peaceful, and positive fashion. If you don't do this now, try to determine why not and fix the situation.

◆ Tell your kids often that you love them. No matter how old they are, hug and kiss them.

Chapter Nine

Testing and Learning

As a teacher, my job and joy was to facilitate learning. I think that is why I enjoyed teaching so much, and still enjoy it today.

My greatest pleasures came when I saw that look on a young person's face that shouted, "I get it!" I loved it when a student came up to me during a science experiment and said, "Mr. Burgett, this really *does* work!" I had a sense of euphoria when after a lesson kids would *feel good* because they could solve the problems or answer the questions.

There are books that talk about the "teaching moment" but I like to think of it as the instant when all previous instruction, all wisdom from past experiences, and all abilities collide at once and metaphorically a light flashes and the student "feels" real learning. The moment is exemplified by a reaction of wonder, satisfaction, or both.

"Mr. Holland's Opus" is a movie in which Richard Dreyfuss plays Glenn Holland, a musician and composer who becomes a teacher to pay the rent and pursue his musical goals. He enters the profession with the thought that teaching will be a moneymaker, but soon he is hooked and discovers that he has the skills needed to change lives. And he likes it.

One character, a redheaded female high school student, comes into Mr. Holland's classroom and says she wants to quit band. Mr. Holland tells her that she is just frustrated because she isn't experiencing success. He talks to her for a while and then asks her to sit and play her instrument. In the moments that follow, the audience sees teaching at its very best. The young girl tries to play a song but gets stuck at the same place each time. Mr. Holland encourages her with a number of different methods, but each fails to get the job done. Finally, he tells her to stop and asks her what she likes best about herself. She shyly says she likes her hair. She says her dad says it reminds him of the sunset. Mr. Holland tells her to close her eyes and play the song from memory. She panics but he says she can do it. She tries but gets stuck once again. He now tells her to close her eyes and play the sunset. She looks at him strangely, and then complies. She plays right through the tough part and stops, opens her eyes, and smiles with that sense of wonder that all teachers strive for. Mr. Holland laughs and says to keep playing. She does, and while doing so she recaptures her confidence.

The next scene shows her playing in the band at high school graduation, in her graduation gown.

The moment in the movie is magic. It is the kind of teaching moment all educators strive for. "Mr. Holland's Opus" shows that special something that we in our profession are blessed to experience.

I have found that a lot of students learn best during the testing process. For that reason I believe testing should be equal parts teaching and assessment, with the emphasis on learning.

I readily admit to being a bit of a rogue when it comes to testing. I liked doing some things my way, especially when it came to testing and assessments. I felt that my concepts worked and that kids did indeed learn while being tested—and learning is what it is all about. So please let me share some of my own personal thoughts about finding that teaching moment during the testing process.

It might be helpful to do some defining before we get too far ahead. When I refer to testing in this chapter I am not referring to standardized tests or state assessments. I am referring to teacher-made or curriculum tests like those found at the end of a chapter. I generally preferred to construct my own tests and I think you will see why.

I strongly believe in the standards movement and I support the umbrella of *No Child Left Behind*. Children should be measured by formal assessments and curriculum should include fundamental standards of learning as developed by the state, regional, or local school systems. There is nothing wrong with reasonable accountability for all children as long as it reflects their abilities or special needs. I also strongly believe that these types of tests (which I will bunch under the heading of "assessments") should be treated seriously and that students should be properly trained in test-taking procedures. Most importantly, they should have learned the material before taking the assessment.

Let me summarize my beliefs with the following statements regarding fundamental responsibilities of teachers:

1. Know the standards you are expected to teach.
2. Understand the curriculum selected.
3. Be able to facilitate learning of the standards.
4. Properly test students' knowledge.
5. Prepare students for assessments.
6. Administer assessments ethically.

This chapter addresses steps 3 and 4 of this list. Again, I believe that learning and testing can be partners.

My idea of a classroom test is not merely a device to measure learning or achievement. A test should be a teaching and learning tool. Time spent testing should also be time spent learning and being motivated, or extending learning opportunities.

A typical classroom process might go something like this. Introduce the topic. Teach the content. Assign homework. Give quizzes or short tests for measurement of progress. Repeat the process until you accumulate enough learning that requires a more comprehensive test, and then keep going until you get to a point where you will review and test over the complete unit of content. This might reflect chapters that become learning units that in turn become nine-week or semester exams.

There is nothing wrong with this process as long as it truly *inspires learning* as well as measuring achievement.

When I taught math it was imperative that every student was able to master each consecutive unit of study since one became the building block for the next. For that reason, homework became a fundamental learning experience and quizzes became important measurements of growth and understanding. I gave quizzes frequently and almost always utilized in-class grading to encourage learning. Let me give you an example.

Let's say the students took a 10-problem quiz. It generally would follow a unit of instruction and maybe a day or two of assignments. Immediately after taking the quiz, students would exchange papers with another student. I had SOP's for all my classes (standard operating procedures) that were clearly defined and numbered. The SOP for grading was that all math quizzes would be graded in ink (all math was done in pencil). The ink could be any color other than red. The grader signed the bottom of the quiz, last page. The grader was responsible to mark the incorrect answers wrong and provide the correct answer. Quizzes were seldom collected until the next day. Students were responsible for taking the quiz home and correcting all mistakes. Corrections had to be done on a separate piece of paper and all work shown in detail. If the problem could be solved without a work process, they were responsible for writing (in sentences) the rationale for the correct answer.

Corrected quizzes were graded 10 out of 10. A corrected quiz was essentially the same grade as a perfect quiz. Every student was expected to turn in a "10" quiz.

Students were expected to retain the corrected quizzes and keep them in a notebook. I told them that the notebook contained all the secret ingredients of any unit test or final exam they would receive in the future. Get it? They were required to take, correct, and keep ongoing assessments as tools for learning.

One of the biggest mysteries to me when I was a student was the lack of follow up that existed in most learning situations. If you "earned" a "C" on a test, for instance, it meant that it was acceptable to learn an average amount of information. My thought was that if it was important enough to teach, it must have been important enough to learn. Many of my own teachers returned tests (or assessments) and that was that. If you missed any questions, so be it. Few made you correct, research, explain, or be accountable for what you missed. This is probably why even today I can't remember where commas go and how or why other basic concepts of grammar function. (Thank God for grammar, spell checkers, and for Mr. B!) Maybe it was also why I really never understood calculus.

When I had a teacher who made me revisit the questions I missed, or had me take assessments a different way, or made testing a learning process, it really substantiated two things— how important the material was and the expectation that I was to learn it!

I remember a junior high science test that involved dissection. Several days before the test we were told about the process, partners were assigned, and we were informed that the only way we could communicate during the test was through writing. We were given a chance to think through the test process. We were also told that if our partner was absent we might be given another at the last minute, or we would take the test individually.

When it came time for the test we gathered in our teams and were given an answer sheet. The lab was set with several stations; each had either a dissection pan containing some poor defunct animal baring its insides, a photo, or a question. We were assembled in a classroom and told that at the "go" we would be asked to move into the lab and stand by one of the stations. We were reminded that no verbal communications would be allowed. We could communicate with our partner only by written notes, sign language, or in some appropriate, non-verbal format. If we talked, we would be removed from the test. We were reminded to put our answers in the right places on the answer sheet since only one of the teams would be starting at number one. We were told that after 60 seconds we would be asked to move, and we should only look at the next station after we were given the signal. We were asked if there were any questions about the instructions.

It was an amazing 25-minute assessment. We were forced to visually identify parts of dissected animals, identify items on photos, and answer some related questions. Each station reflected what we had studied and done in previous labs and in the classroom. Each team would share the same score.

I think I valued that experience more than any assessment I had previously taken. It was real. It reflected what we had learned. It was a mirror image of the quizzes we had previously taken. It required test-taking savvy, communication skills, and knowledge of the topic. Those who had taken the test seriously whipped through it. The instructor, a genius in my opinion, did an excellent job of preparing us for the exam. In fact, he did an excellent job of creating a learning situation.

When the exam was done, he graded it on the spot. It was objective so all he had to do was compare our answer sheet to a code of numbers and letters, and he had half the number of students to grade since we were in pairs. As soon as we received our grade, we were to return to the stations we missed and make an effort to correct our answers, since we still didn't know the real answer. We could collect information, make a drawing, review previous quizzes or notes, use our textbook, anything, but we could not talk. We would receive no credit for the test until the corrected answer sheet was returned with written justification for corrected answers. Finally, everything written we turned in was subject to what he called the "English Factor" (the EF). That meant there was a reduction in possible points for grammar or spelling errors! That's right, he graded the content and the form of every written statement. Missing capitals, no punctuation, improper grammar, misspelled words, all yielded a loss of total points from the answer. His rationale was that proper communication skills were among the most important things we would ever learn!

He was a master teacher. Not only did we learn the content (and from the assessment of the content), we learned how to communicate. And it was *fun*!

I stole the EF concept from this master teacher and used it myself when teaching science, math, social studies, and physical education. I also carbon copied many of his test procedures. *Good teachers want to be copied.*

It wasn't until a long time later that I also learned that he used what I call hi-lo "mose pairing." That is my unscientific terminology for putting two people together, whenever possible, who can teach each other. "Hi mose" is short for "highly motivated" and "lo mose" means someone "less motivated." Now don't be confused with honor roll students helping struggling students. Mose pairing (as I call it) is when you match any two students who will learn from each other. They may be friends and both be honor students, but one may coast by and the other may work hard for every grade he or she gets. They may both be slower students, but one is aggressive about learning and other could care less. The aggressive one won't let the nonchalant student pull the grade down.

A question always comes up: How do you prevent one student from doing all the work? That brings up what I call the "WTW." WTW simply means "Work Together Warranty." It is implemented with a post-test WTW assessment. It may be one question, ten questions, or no questions—the option is up to the instructor. It works this way. After the teamed assessment is complete, each individual may be asked to take a repeat mini-exam. If he or she misses any questions on this exam, the deduction is taken off the teamed assessment. Thus if both parties have not *learned* the material, both will be penalized. A good teacher can easily tell if one partner is pulling the weight for the team and can remind the team of the WTW. A one- or two-question follow-up assessment is a good way to keep everyone on track. Best of all, it works!

Teaming has always been a proven way of teaching. Team testing is also a great way to promote learning, develop communication skills, and promote cooperation.

Assessment types should of course vary. Team (mose pairing) tests should not be the only type of test you use. I preferred a variety of testing situations to fairly collect data on achievement and learning.

On the side or bottom of every textbook for new teachers should be this statement: *"Warning, the procedures outlined in this book will not work for every teacher in every circumstance. And you will not die a premature death if you experience failure individualizing the material. If something doesn't work for you, alter it, try it again, and if it still doesn't work, try something different. The key is to find a way to teach that promotes learning."*

That warning also fits for creative test making, test giving, and test learning. What worked for me, and for dozens of other teachers, may not work for you. Over the course of my career I have given literally hundreds of different types of tests and assessments. Some worked like charms to enhance learning. Some were creative disasters. However, *I learned* from each experience.

Here are a few more testing situations that you may want to consider:

If you are teaching a long unit of study, begin the program by giving the *unit exam* to each student. Carefully change the "real" questions with ones that are very similar by altering the question a bit, changing the numbers, etc. Tell them that essentially the exam they see is quite similar to the exam you will administer at the end of the unit of study. Tell them that putting this exam in their notebooks is required; they should refer to it when they do their homework and for spot quizzes or weekly tests. At the end of the unit they should have completed this exam ahead of time as a study tool. Make this what I called a required though not necessarily collected assignment.

Is this teaching to the test? *Absolutely!* However, if the test measures what you want to teach, what's the problem? Will kids focus on this exam more than on the unit of study? No way, unless you don't require homework, give additional tests and quizzes along the way, and have outside work (reading, projects, papers, etc.) to supplement the unit. If the only thing they do for six weeks is read and practice and take the unit exam, then this may be a concern.

My goal when submitting a unit exam on the first day is to outline the unit, set up what is ahead for the next six weeks, introduce terms and concepts they will learn, and, hopefully, spark their interest. This closely follows Madeline Hunter's model of a perfect lesson plan: objectives, standards, anticipatory set, etc. It's actually a cool way to get a unit started.

There's a kicker too. I have ended units by telling kids to be sure to bring their notebooks with them since they may need to refer to something in the notebook. Then I have asked them to remove the unit exam and turn it in. Surprise! Some of them really are shocked when the "required but not necessarily collected assignment" becomes the real unit exam. Naturally I give them time to complete or check it, but the students who have followed the plan and have been answering the questions all along are done. They have been learning as they were doing so the test is an accurate measure of knowledge. Risky? I never thought so because of all the other measurements along the way and the level of work that was always required.

Sometimes I did what they expected and gave them a similar, but not exact, unit exam. Sometimes I let them use any resource other than their notebook. Sometimes I let them compare their finished exam with their Mose partner, reminding them that if they elected to do this, the WTW factor would be applied. Confusing? Not to them, not to me, and not if the process is clear and the objective is always put in front of them—that the most important part of their job (going to school) is to *learn*.

I also used (1) take-home exams, (2) make-your-own exams, (3) make an exam for your MOSE partner and bring it the next day and each of you will take each other's exam, and (4) a variety of forms of exams.

Sometimes I would give a three-question exam asking them to explain how they knew something was true. In other words, the process was the focus rather than the answer. Sometimes I gave matching exams where the column of letter answers actually spelled out something. At times I gave exams that included a trick question, and if they guessed which was the trick question they got bonus points. I frequently gave exams that had funny choices along with the real ones.

Sometimes I gave exams that also dealt with following instructions. An example is an exam that starts with bold and underlined instructions that say "read every question on this exam before you answer any of them." And then somewhere near the end of the exam one of the questions would end with a statement that said "If you have not answered any question yet, raise your hand for a surprise." I would then come to that student and give them five bonus points for following directions. What did that measure? It measured their capacity to follow directions, and it was also fun. Kids love things like that.

Many times, if the tests were totally objective (multiple choice, true/false, matching, etc.), I would give various forms of the exam, moving the order of questions around so that neighboring students did not have the same test (although they had the same questions). This certainly put a cork in eyeball cheating.

The list of test options is endless. And test construction can be a lot of fun.

Another thing I did was develop and maintain a vocabulary list. Remember, I mostly taught science and math, but I used the EF process no matter what I taught. If we had a new word, or there was some word we used that seemed to be strange to many, I would post it on the board. They were required to add it to their notebook. The definition and spelling of that word would find its way to a quiz or test, guaranteed. They knew that, so the vocabulary list was no surprise. English teachers loved me, at least most of the time!

Let's talk a few minutes about grading. I worked in a system that at one time adopted a district-wide grading scale. You may not agree with what I am about to say and you would certainly have a long list of people on your side, but this is my book so here goes.

I don't like standardized grading scales. To me they say that I'm incapable of determining, through my own process, the level of achievement a student has reached. That directly questions my own professional abilities. Sorry, but that's how I feel.

However, and there is always a "however" in life, I complied because I was a team player. Boards, administrators, educational specialists in tall towers, or (God forbid) from Washington D.C. sometimes knew more than I did, so I complied. Somehow I managed to mathematically add a factor to my own way of grading that, in the end, made my "A" grade meet their 93-100 range, or whatever. It wasn't worth the battle of being non-compliant. But, in the long run, I determined the range based on what the student *learned* and *earned*.

I firmly believe that grades are motivators as well as achievement measurements. Let the state assessment exam, or the standardized test process, measure the kid's ability compared to a group of millions of like humanoids. I measured their day-to-day learning based on who they were, how much they worked, and what they learned. If an average kid ended up with "A" in my class, halleluiah! If a genius ended up with "C," I hope it was a wake-up call. I tried my best to encourage and facilitate learning beyond formal grades on report cards. I did this successfully because I was fair and honest, I communicated and recorded information with a great deal of articulation and understanding, and I never wavered from the focus of learning.

I treated daily assignments as basic requirements of the job. I would tell my students that I didn't get bonus points for coming to work, but I did get punished if I didn't do my job. I told them that the same concept applied to their "job" of getting an education.

Another heresy, and again you don't have to agree with what I am about to share, but please hear me out. I gave daily assignments a grade of zero. In my grade book (or on my computer grading program) when a student did their daily assignment and corrected all missed problems or questions, they received a zero. I treated it as basic, fundamental, required work, nothing more. If, however, they turned in daily assignments that were not completed, weren't corrected, or weren't even started, they could lose up to 10 points for that single assignment.

The negative score would be added in with their quiz and test scores at the end of the grading unit. Yikes! Daily work now had real value! You weren't rewarded for doing what was required but you were penalized for not doing what was expected. *Sounds like real life.*

The key to making this work was the individual conferences I had with kids who racked up negative homework points, the calls to parents, the report to their advisor about needed special help, or whatever it took to keep them on track. That was my job if I was serious about them *learning*.

Here is a sample phone call home. "Mr. Johnson, sorry I missed you but I want you to know that I have talked with Jimmy about missing two daily assignments in science. Now he just missed the third one within two weeks. Please talk with Jimmy and let him explain to you about how daily assignments are graded. Please understand that I cannot measure how much he is learning if he doesn't meet his daily requirements. If you need more information from me, I am available from 9:12-10:00 a.m. every morning at 654--------. Please feel free to give me a call. Thanks for your help."

This call takes about 30 seconds. I usually tried to make it during the day when there was about a 90% chance that no one was home so I could leave it on the answering machine. I preferred to leave it on the answering machine in the hope that Jimmy and/or Mom and Dad would all hear it. I always made a note in my book that I had made the call, and I always asked the student the next day if they had discussed it. This covered me in many ways. Communication usually gets the job done.

Learning incentives is the final topic in this chapter. You might call this extra credit or bonus points. Whatever it is called, it should be used to enhance motivation, expand learning, and supplement daily requirements, not replace them.

I like learning incentives. Kids like them too. If a student wants to learn more, do more, take an alternative route to learning, think more, or be more creative, then what's wrong with learning incentives?

At the end of many tests I gave a "Learning Incentive" question. If they did it and got it right, they earned extra points. Extra credit? Sure! But they weren't easy, they weren't giveaways, and they were always designed to challenge the level of learning. Also, they weren't graded if the test wasn't completed or daily requirements for that unit weren't meeting expectations. In other words, if a student had any negative points for daily work, learning incentives were not applicable.

I also used a list of alternatives as learning incentives, such as (1) read a book from a list of approved titles and give a written or oral report, (2) design a sign, create a handout, or make a poster/bulletin board that explains a concept or explains an idea, (3) develop a lesson to be used to teach one of the concepts, (4) build a model, create a website, or find a list of related sites on the web, or, (5) create a proposal for a learning incentive of your own.

I found that if you make the topic interesting enough, teach the basics well enough, and blend in a lot of fun and amazement, kids not only learn, they want to learn more.

Teachers will change lives when a student discovers the excitement and enjoyment of learning. Well-crafted lesson plans are one way of doing this, but combining good instruction with testing that also enhances learning is even better. Does it take more time to do the things listed in this chapter? Of course it does. Is it worth it? You bet.

Creative testing enhances learning. Good teachers focus on learning. Good teachers change lives!

◆ When determining a student's grade, if you are on the line and decide to give the student the higher grade, share that decision with him/her and give the student the opportunity to know that you have faith in their work.

◆ Incorporate reading and writing into all subjects. Utilize the EF (English Factor) in everything you teach.

◆ If you are teaching new material, forget the idea that you only need to be prepared one day ahead of your class. Two days is minimum. They know when you are faking it and they will take advantage of an unprepared teacher.

◆ Tests are great ways to teach, but they can also be ways to have fun while teaching. Not all test questions need to be boring and informational. Throw in one or two that are just plain fun.

◆ Evaluate often. Practice the theory of teach, assess, re-teach, reassess. Give as much feedback as you can. Don't count every assessment, but use them to teach the topic.

◆ Try test teams. Give the test one day to a preset team of students to practice, discuss, work, and peer-coach. The next day actually give the same test (maybe rearrange the questions) to individuals to do on their own for a grade. Don't forget that the purpose of a test is not just to measure knowledge but also to facilitate learning.

◆ Keep them busy with a variety of activities. Concentrating exclusively on just one thing during a class is boring for some students. The most productive periods are those where the kids are so involved that they are surprised to learn that the period is already over. A mix of such things as a short video, some discussion, and a worksheet would be better, for example, than watching a video the entire period.

◆ Vary activities and use "hands-on" as much as possible. Example: 20% of the social studies credits in one high school are earned by something called "Discovery Credits." The mandatory credits come from building medieval castles, giving oral reports, visiting lead mines, touring museums, interviewing World War II veterans, etc.

◆ Use highly motivated students to tutor less motivated students. For example, during a practice spelling test, select one student who earns 100% to help the others with that practice test. Involve as many students as possible. This encourages them to study harder for this test.

◆ Set achievement incentives such as "Anyone who gets a 100% on the pretest doesn't have to take the real test." Then use those students as tutors during the lesson and offer bonus points to the tutors if their "students" do well.

◆ Let students take tests when they are ready, and reward early achievers. Students who pass these timed tests early become coaches for others, they help make flash cards, give quizzes, etc.

◆ Vary the kinds of test questions and situations so you tap different abilities. Scores of options are available on the Internet or by talking with peers.

◆ Base grades on units completed rather than on numbers or percentages. De-emphasize formal, traditional testing and use project and/or unit completions to determine part of student grades. An A, B, etc., is earned for successfully completing a predetermined number of units. Examples:

- Papers or tests—each paper or test earning 80% or better equals one unit, 95% or better equals 1.5 units.
- Each successfully completed demonstration equals one unit, like a "Show and Tell" report.
- Poems of a certain length equal one unit.

"Keep on going and the chances are you will stumble on something, perhaps even when you are least expecting it. I have never heard of anyone stumbling on something sitting down."

Charles F. Kettering
1876-1958

Chapter Ten

Expectations and Environment

This chapter talks about some of the prime "meat" of teaching. Things like rules, the learning environment, handling new students, setting expectations for learning, and more.

It doesn't replace solid educational research or what was taught at the university. Rather, what I'm sharing here was learned through the school of experience either first hand or from some very, very successful educators. So let's take off our coat and stay awhile. We have a lot of important things to cover.

Let's start with one of the fundamentals of teaching—classroom rules. Many folks live under an orderly set of parameters and they want that to prevail everywhere in their lives. There is nothing wrong with order and/or organization.

I too like order and a set of understandable rules. Kind of like traffic control. I also like realistic and workable parameters. For instance, I know that the speed limit in my home state on the Interstates is usually 65. I also know that in many areas if you drive at 70 you will never be stopped, and if you drive at 65 you had best be in the right lane because the other cars will run you over if you aren't. A realistic and working parameter is to set the cruise control at 70 and enjoy life.

If the rules are "no talking" when someone else is talking and a kid, Billy, leans over and says five words to his neighbor, once, I probably won't react with a dire punishment, following the Lee Cantor list of checkmarks set by the

District Disciplinary Annihilation Corps. I will probably give Billy a look and keep on teaching.

If Jamie comes into class 37 seconds late, after I have escorted what I thought was the last student through the doorway and I've started the class with a positive note (thanks for the example, Mr. B), I will probably ask Jamie to see me for a minute after class. I'll ask her why she was late, and if she gives me a reasonable excuse (bathroom, talking to a teacher, forgot a book, broke up with a short-term boyfriend during passing period), I may be humane and say okay this time, or I may say that this is the second time this semester and the next time she will be asked to stay after school, or what ever the rules are. I won't send her immediately to the assistant principal's tardy-execution squad. My point? Be fair, not crazy. Set up rules and expectations that are realistic and treat others with some degree of reality and respect.

Mike Klippert (you'll meet him in the Cast of Characters) always demonstrated this fundamental of classroom control. He treated all kids with respect and they responded by treating everyone else with respect. It works.

So what should the rules be? Or should there be a list of rules? Are rules necessary? Should your classroom rules differ from the district rules?

Every teacher has classroom rules. Some of them make sense, some don't. The key to successful classroom rules falls within these parameters:

1. They must be known and understood.
2. They must be reasonable and make sense.
3. They must be administered consistently.
4. They must be enforceable—and enforced.

Meet these criteria and you're well on the way to having a problem-free environment that is conducive to learning. Problem-free means that you won't need the rules you have!

My personal ideas about rules? Rules don't create or establish order in a classroom. The teacher does that. Rules don't keep kids from getting in trouble. Active, interesting, well-planned classroom management does that. Rules won't make a kid learn; they will only help you maintain an environment for learning. Rules, by themselves, won't bring you respect. Respect has to be earned. Rules are necessary but they are not the panacea to changing lives.

That said, let me put my rules in the right perspective. I'll never tell you that I was the greatest teacher in the world, because I wasn't. But I will tell you that I seldom dealt with disciplinary problems. I worked in systems that had district rules, suggested classroom rules, and organizational procedures. I followed them because I was a good soldier and a team member, and it is the right thing to do. But within the walls of my classroom I handled things before they ever became subject to systematic scrutiny.

To begin with, I made it clear to students that I would treat them with respect and would *assume* they knew how to act appropriately. I made it clear that no matter what their history, their status, their involvement in anything, their academic record, or anything else, when they walked into my room they did so with a clean slate and to me they were all human beings worthy of respect. I told them I wouldn't be using inappropriate language or behavior, and I *expected* the same from them.

I set the standard from day one (on day one) and referred to this standard and double-edged sword of respect many, many times. I complimented and reinforced excellent behavior and used the word "proud" often. I built within them a sense of ownership of the classroom and an understanding that they were special and appreciated. I spent more time on this than I ever did on discipline. Kids respected me; more important, I respected them.

Once I remember hearing a seventh grader using the "F" word in the hallway between classes. I was in the door waiting for my kids to arrive and he was walking by and pushed some buddy (not a fight, but in fun) and called him an "F-head." Our "instructions" as teachers were that all students belonged to every teacher and if we witnessed an infraction of the rules we were to handle it no matter where or when. To every rule I always add this codicil, "...using common sense and in an appropriate manner." So I merely walked toward the student, whose name I did not know, tapped him on the shoulder, and asked him to step aside. Quietly, as other students passed, I told him that I heard him use an inappropriate word that described his friend's head. He semi-smiled but he also lowered his head, knowing that the gauntlet was about to drop. I asked him if he used this word frequently. The boy amazed me. He said, "No, sir, I don't. My parents would kill me if they knew I used it. I know it's not right. I'm sorry." I told him that we both knew he was old enough to know the word and use it, and since he had accomplished that feat, he needed to demonstrate his maturity now by *not* using it. Not using inappropriate words was more impressive in the long run than using them. I asked him if he understood what I meant. He said he did. I then asked him his name and told him to stop by my classroom after school before he got on the bus. I didn't say anything else. He thanked me and said he would.

I never told him my name, or where my classroom was. He seemed responsible, and I had his name. Later that day I saw the principal in the hallway and asked him if he knew the boy. He responded that he did, he was a good kid, feisty, fun, and had supportive parents who were divorced. The principal said that the boy spent time with each parent on a regular basis. That was the end of the discussion. For a few steps at least, I walked in the boy's moccasins.

At the end of the day the boy stopped by my classroom. He stood by my desk as I finished up with a few other students. When everyone else left, I asked him what he thought I should do about the situation. He said he knew that I would have to report him to the principal and he apologized. I then told him that the principal had told me what a good kid he was, that he was fun and had good parents. I then said, "It sounds to me like you know what is appropriate and what isn't. I also appreciated your apology. The next time I see you in the hall I hope the first thing I hear is 'Hi, Mr. Burgett!' Now this is what I want you to do for me—work a bit harder tonight on your homework! Go home, and work hard at what *not* to say." He smiled, I smiled, and the fact that he had to think about his punishment for getting caught all day was sufficient punishment in itself. We ended the situation on a positive note. He was reinforced for apologizing, respected for his behavior after I stopped him in the hall, and had a greater appreciation for the principal knowing how he felt about the boy and his parents. Did I follow the rules? Probably not, because I never "turned him in" for a proper lashing and check accumulation. Did I solve the problem? Absolutely. Every time he saw me he would say hello. When he became my student we already had a positive and instant bond—and mutual respect.

Had the principal told me the boy was not to be trusted, was a junior con man, or was someone who needed discipline, I probably would have done things differently. I may have asked him to see me every day for a week, or to stay after school one night, and we would have talked. I would have tried to turn him around and would have crafted some kind of "learning" discipline. But that's me. My method might not work for you. The point is simply this: one size does not fit all when it comes to discipline. Sometimes you have to measure the criminal before you size up the penalty.

I have known hundreds of teachers most of whom had their own set of classroom rules. In one situation we were required to have our classroom rules in writing and a copy given to each student and sent home for a signature. Of course a copy went to the main office to be filed by the rules protection agency, or whomever. Some folks felt more at ease using a progressive list of consequences attached to the rules.

For instance, maybe the rules included things like no horseplay, no running, no gum chewing, no inappropriate use of language, no fighting, raising your hand to be recognized, no talking unless given permission, and so on... The list of consequences may be related to accumulating checkmarks. For example, the first time you are caught breaking a rule you get your name on the board. The second offense earns a checkmark. If you get caught again, you get another checkmark. At the end of the day, week, month (whatever), you have to meet the consequence for the number of checkmarks. One mark may simply be a warning, two may mean a detention after school or in some in-school prison, three may mean contact with the home, four may mean removal of a leg or arm by the Dean of students—for repeat offenders, any remaining limbs.

You may think I'm kidding about rules becoming so formal and complicated. I'm not. I see it all the time and it drives me nuts. It is all I can do not to ask, "Who brings their horse to school and plays with it?" Or, "Who has the time to manage checkmarks and all the nonsense related to these formal and absolutely subjective processes?"

The most effective teachers I have ever met did not have to fool with this type of process. They demanded appropriate behavior, taught appropriate behavior, and managed inappropriate behavior. They used classic teaching principles such as proximity, visual and physical contact without a disruption in teaching, and a variety of other disciplinary approaches before actually doing anything such as sending the kid off to the office Gestapo or calling home. An example? Easy. Here are a few to consider:

- Paige is constantly talking to her friend Vanessa while you are teaching. You give Paige the evil eye and keep teaching. She stops. Case closed.

- Paige is constantly talking to her friend Vanessa while you are teaching. You give Paige the evil eye and keep teaching. She doesn't stop. You walk over to her, stand by her, and keep teaching. She stops talking. After class you call her aside and thank her for stopping her conversation with Vanessa; that you appreciate the fact that she respected your request for attention while you are teaching. Case closed.

- Paige is constantly talking to her friend Vanessa while you are teaching. You give Paige the evil eye and keep teaching. She doesn't stop. You walk over to her, stand by her, and keep teaching. She stops for a minute until you walk away, then starts talking again. You walk back over, keep teaching, but this time simply put your hand on her back, or tap her lightly on the shoulder. She looks at you and you move your head slightly saying "no." After class you call her aside and thank her for realizing that it was disruptive when she talked to Vanessa. Case closed.

• Paige is constantly talking to her friend Vanessa when you are teaching. You give Paige the evil eye, you engage in "proximity" and even give her the "stop talking" visual cue, but she keeps on talking. You have tried three different approaches, but none have worked. You now have a choice to make. Do you interrupt your teaching to talk to her? Do you wait until after class to talk to her? Do you put her name on the board and start writing checks behind it? Do you wait until you stop actively teaching and deal with this during individual practice time? Every situation differs. If Paige is really disrupting the classroom, you need to handle it now. If Paige is in need of a minor adjustment, it's probably best to wait. No matter when, or how, you need to communicate to Paige these things:

* I gave you a look that should have indicated to you that your talking was both disruptive to my teaching and disrespectful.

* I stood by you, hoping you would know that your continued talking was still disrespectful to me as a teacher, and to the other students, and was preventing Vanessa from listening to the lesson. I even got your attention and shook my head no, asking you to stop.

Then ask Paige what it was she didn't understand about any of those actions?

Hopefully, she now understands and maybe even apologizes, so you can move on. If not, you may need to employ a consequence or *real* threat from your bag of discipline.

A possible consequence is telling Paige that you may need to assign her a seat to help her not be tempted to talk to her friends, or you may have her come in after school to do some school work, or you may need to call her mom or dad to find out what they can suggest to get her attention, etc. "Real" threats are when you tell Paige that if she continues to talk in class again, there will be no warnings and consequences will be enforced.

This is the key. If you make a threat and don't do it, you are just like the weak parent who says if you don't finish your dinner you won't get dessert, yet the kid knows dessert will happen no matter what, how, or when. Real threats are followed by real consequences and kids *know* that you mean real business. Kids actually respect you more when you do what you say you will do, if it is reasonable and responsible. You see, kids want order and discipline.

You can have all the rules in the world and they will hold as much weight as a bag full of hot air if they don't make sense, aren't understood, or, worst of all, aren't enforced.

It's not the rules that make the difference, it's the ruler.

Before we leave rules, let me share my personal process with you. It may not work for you but it worked well for me.

I had one classroom rule. This was the one I sent home and had signed when I worked at a building that required it.

Be cool, not cruel.

That was it. My one and only rule. Oh yes, I had to explain it about a billion times over the years to parents, anal-retentive administrators, and even to teachers. The only group that seemed to understand it right away was the kids. I used this guiding principle for students in grades 5-12 and I always opened the year with a brief explanation and example of the rule. It went something like this.

"I know that everyone in this room knows the difference between right and wrong and between what is appropriate (the right thing to do) and what is inappropriate (the wrong thing to do). Because of that we don't need a long list of rules telling us how to behave. So we have one rule to follow that will cover everything we do in and out of the classroom, wherever we go, and whatever we do as a class or as individuals from this class. That rule is, 'Be cool, not cruel.'

"You will determine how we administer that rule. For example, do I need to tell anyone that hitting someone over the head with a chair is inappropriate? That type of behavior is not cool, but very cruel. You would be breaking our one and only rule and would have to face a consequence. Does everyone understand?

"How about talking when someone else is talking?"

(Depending on the age group, this might provoke an interesting discussion. Someone might say that if the class is engaged in small group activities, many may be talking at once, so there it is appropriate. Together, the class realizes that a general rule doesn't fit all circumstances! This is just what you want to have happen!)

"As we conduct class there will be situations that we need to discuss and define. Together we will determine if the activity in question is cool or cruel; also, if it should or should not be continued. You will have a say but, as the paid leader and protector of your rights and safety, I will have the final vote. Since we are all reasonable, intelligent, and cool people, there is no doubt we can manage and govern ourselves with dignity."

Kids love this approach and it works. The only concern is that kids will be tougher rule makers in most situations than I might be.

If the discussion turns to consequences, I always tell them that consequences are inconsequential if everyone is cool and not cruel, but if the situation does come up that requires a consequence, that will be my responsibility. The focus is to establish a learning environment that allows students to grow, to work together, and to experience a positive (cool) atmosphere. The focus is on learning. Learning changes lives.

One final thought on discipline and rules. Any teacher who has a problem in this arena should seek help. A mentor, a visitor to the classroom, video taping several lessons for personal (or professional) review, or any diagnostic evaluation of procedures and processes can help a struggling teacher discover what is working and what isn't. If a teacher spends more time on discipline and classroom management than on teaching, they are missing the enjoyment of teaching. If one student, or even a couple, take more time than they deserve for behavioral management, then seek new strategies. A simple solution is to see if there is a teacher who does not have the same type of problems with the same students and find out what works for them.

Let's shift from rules and discipline to organization.

I can picture in my head three classrooms as clearly as I can see the screen on my iMac. One is an old junior high science room in a very old school building. The other is an early elementary grade classroom, again in an old school building. The third is a special education classroom for intermediate grade students in a relatively new building.

In all cases the schools themselves were well maintained, neat, orderly, and safe. And, in each case, if you walked into any of the three mentioned classrooms your first assumption would be that you were in a classroom supply storage room. One even had a room within the room for kids to read in.

I would rank the three teachers who "owned" these rooms as above average in teaching abilities. One I would even rank as exceptional. Their rooms, however, were disasters. Two of the three were well organized and the teacher knew in a heartbeat where everything was and could find a handout, overhead, game, or book instantly. The third teacher probably had a hard time finding her car keys at the end of the day.

Even though the three teachers were good teachers, they lost immediate credibility with everyone because their rooms looked dangerous, disorganized, and inappropriate. My point? What you see is not always what you get, but how it is perceived by others always affects potential outcome. No matter how good these teachers were, they could have been more effective if their rooms were more appropriate. Organization, real or perceived, makes a difference.

One of the most brilliant men I ever met worked for a State Board of Education. He was also one of the most disorganized. His office was a total disaster. His behavior was also inappropriate at times, and he looked like a slob. He retained his job for many years because his brain was more valued than the impression he left. Had I been his boss I would have suggested a lobotomy, kept his brain, and fired the rest of him. He was a visual and professional disgrace.

Teaching is a public profession. It demands appropriate and ethical behavior. We should expect teachers to demonstrate to young students organized, reasonable, and respectful behavior. If universities and businesses want to hire the unorthodox, that is fine, but in my personal opinion, pre-K to 12 educational institutions should demand an environment that demonstrates high expectations, organization, and appropriateness. Is this "old school" thinking? Maybe it is, but I believe it is "best school" thinking as well.

Here is my personal concept of an exciting, inviting, and motivating classroom. It is first of all clean. Not void of activity, but clean. It has signs of learning. Things on the walls, things on the shelves, evidence of projects, group activities, files, technology, screens, projectors, and action. It's neither sterile nor predictable. You can "feel" teaching. Outside the classroom should be the teacher's name and subject or grade, and, hopefully, a welcome sign. Inside, if it is a self-contained classroom, something about each student. If it is single-subject classroom, I hope to see something about the topic or subject. Something that comes alive and says *learning takes place here!* Even if it is a classroom occupied by a traveling teacher, there should be something to make the classroom environment exciting.

I once knew a traveling music teacher who had a cart she wheeled from room to room that looked like something from the TV show *Pimp My Ride*. She also had taken one of those yellow "wet floor" plastic placards and had a message painted on it that said *"Sounds of Music Inside*—Take a Peek!" and she would put it outside the classroom in the hallway. When anyone did take a peek, she had the kids primed to say in unison (to her visual cue) "welcome to our world of learning" and then she gave the visitor a preplanned medley of songs that lasted about a minute. It was absolutely magical and the kids (and visitors) loved it! Talk about environment!

Want to know what your classroom looks like? Ask a third-party volunteer to walk into several rooms in your school (including yours) and to share their immediate reaction. You may even prompt them as to whether they sense excitement, learning, comfort, organization, etc. in what they see.

Environmentally a classroom should be comfortable, clean, organized, and conducive to learning. This means it should work. Heating and air conditioning should be manageable and workable. If the room simply doesn't get cool or warm enough because of the infrastructure of the building, then adjust by having kids dress appropriately and make the best of the situation, always reminding the administration of your needs but not being a pain about something you or they may not be able to control.

There is no excuse for inadequate lighting or outlets that don't work. Make a fuss over those things. If window shades don't work and they can't afford to replace them, find an alternative that you can use (decorated drop cloths, drapes, etc.) until you can get shades. If desks are broken or seats can't be adjusted, rattle cages with maintenance or the shop classes. Remember that the squeaky wheel gets the grease—but squeak appropriately and for the right reasons. Students learn better when the classroom is functional, comfortable, and appropriate. Make that a primary goal. No one will argue with you if you are reasonable and have best learning conditions as your focus.

Let me add a potpourri of additional thoughts.

• First comes dress. We have turned the corner in this country when it comes to casual dress. The days of suits, ties, heels, and dresses as required teacher dress may be history, but jeans, exposed skin, cleavage, flip-flops, and sweat suits do not establish the right atmosphere. Even the business world defines "business casual" better than that. If we expect kids to respect us, we need to respect the profession. I know I am treading on thin water when I even hint that there should be a dress code for professional educators—because there *shouldn't* be one. There shouldn't be a dress code not because of personal rights but because as a professional educator we should know what appropriate, professional dress should be. Licensed, certified, college graduate teachers should not need to be told how to dress or behave; it should inherently be part of the position.

• At the beginning of the year have a program in place for students who are new to your school. If they are all new, maybe conduct a tour of the facility and introduce them to people who will serve them. Also have a program in place for welcoming new students during the school year. You may want to involve your current students in developing the program. A simple discussion based on the question, "If you were a new student to our school, what would be helpful to you?" would get them involved (create ownership) in a successful plan.

• No matter what the grade level or subject, kids like visitors who are interesting. Invite mini-lecturers to talk to your kids. I know one very creative kindergarten teacher (you will meet her in the Cast of Characters chapter) who invites the building custodian in as a mini-lecturer when she introduces the letter "T" to her kids. He brings his box and belt of tools and talks about them (and finds lots of "T" words to share).

Here is a tip for using a mini-lecturer. Give them the last 15 minutes of the period. Ask them to bring something to show. Offer to make a handout for them. If they are boring, nervous, or a total disaster, you will only lose 15 minutes! If they are outstanding, interesting, and/or a massive hit, you can invite them back for more. Make their topic and presentation meaningful to what you are teaching.

I remember when we were doing proofs in geometry and a kid asked the perennial question, "Who uses this stuff anyway?" I invited a civil engineer to come to class, dressed in his work boots. He brought a laser scope, tripod, and pictures of a bridge he was working on. He talked about his math background, degrees, and how much money he made. It was fantastic.

• Consider using alternative learning sites that don't require transportation or a field trip. Once a house went on the market next door to the school. I asked the superintendent if my class could take advantage of the house and use it as an alternative learning site. I first had to define alternative learning site and then agree to 10,314 conditions. I suggested that we would take measurements of the house and use it literally as a hands-on lab for determining such things as how much wall paper it would take to remodel certain rooms, how much paint, how much carpeting, and how many ping pong balls it would take to fill the house, top to bottom (to help determine the size of the HVAC system it would need for air conditioning and heating). I suggested we might also determine how much concrete it would take to build a patio, and talk about things such as building codes, math use in the workplace, etc. The superintendent asked me the most reasonable question in response. He asked, "How can I get the real estate office and owner to agree to this request?" I responded that we could work with them in developing an article for the newspaper with photos of the kids in the house. The article could praise the broker for making this a learning opportunity for our kids.

It happened just as requested and it was a win-win for everyone. We had two weeks in our lab before the house was sold. I think the article even helped sell the house!

The alternative learning sites available within walking distance to most schools are there and can make learning interesting. Alternative learning sites even exist within the school building. Keep reading...

• Once, when we were studying the ear in seventh-grade science, I noticed how under-excited the kids were to look at the ear in the book and on the wall chart. I had a small brain spasm and on a whim I called the office to see if the small gym was available for use during that class. It was, so I had all my students line up and walk there. I divided the class into two parts. One went up to the balcony and watched the second group. I then assigned each student a "role" in the experience. One kid was the hammer, some were auditory nerves, some formed the outer ear, etc. I then orchestrated them into position, placing them on the floor of the gym according to what they did.

I grabbed a playground ball and assigned one kid as the "bowler." When everyone was in position, the bowler rolled a playground ball (sound waves) toward the back of a kid cradled inside the outline of the outer ear. The target was the eardrum. This eardrum kid, after he was hit by the rolling ball, tapped another student (who was the hammer), that moved another part (the anvil), that hit the next kid (the stirrup), which eventually resulted in auditory nerves that got up and ran to the wall that served as the brain.

We watched how the ear worked. We experienced it. We used the gym and a playground ball to replicate a human organ. When the group on the floor had demonstrated the hearing process a few times, I had the kids from the balcony come down and the kids on the floor go up, and in the process every kid was to transfer their part to another student. The balcony kids came down and got into position and, after some minor adjustments, put on the demo for the kids in the balcony. How long did all this take? In total, about half the class period. Then we all returned to the classroom and each student wrote a paragraph about what it was like to be the part they played. They had to write it as if they were the outer ear, etc.

Year after year kids looked forward to this experience! Today, eons later, when I see these same folks (now mature adults) they tell me how much fun it was to be the stirrup or eardrum. Alternative learning sites can make *learning* really fun and meaningful.

• Mastery should determine movement. As mentioned in previous chapters, one of my biggest frustrations with teaching (really, with teachers) is movement before mastery. How can we really start teaching at level 2 until the student understands level 1? How can we move to another topic if it depends on the basic understanding of what was previously taught?

Master teachers (those who change lives positively and promote learning) have learned the importance of teaching mastery before moving on. Assessments, testing, and practical applications, along with insight and plain old intuition, help the master teacher understand if mastery has been reached and what degree of mastery is necessary. However, with all that said, we all know that many teachers teach, test, and move on without any regard (or with limited regard) to who gets lost in the process. Expectations of mastery should be essential elements of the teaching process.

• Homework is not an option. Good teachers set realistic standards of homework. Good teachers understand the level of their students, the pressures of unrealistic expectations, and what it takes to achieve mastery learning. Effective, life-changing teachers remind kids that school is their "work" and that some obligations are absolutely essential to success. Homework is one of those obligations. But good teachers also make success a valued and rewarding goal. They make learning a desired outcome. They bring to the table passion, excitement, creativity, and motivation. If work is boring, then the results may be mediocre at best. Work has to be challenging and rewarding. Homework has to be expected, but also appreciated. Good teachers make this happen.

• Parents can be a royal pain in the tush. They can also be exceptionally helpful. Most are so busy making enough money to support the family and trying to do what's best for their kids, that they often don't have the time to become overly involved.

No matter how busy parents are, like us they don't like surprises. A parent opening a report card and discovering that their honor roll student has earned a "C" can be as dangerous to any teacher's well-being as a parent who discovers an "F" without prior warning. A simple note or call reporting that Beulah has bombed her biology exam and is quickly descending toward grade level quicksand is a good way to get Mommy and Daddy involved in some basic Beulah bolstering. Just as important is a quick call or note that Beulah just earned a brilliant B on her botany test is making great progress this nine-week term, and you wanted to share your appreciation for her good work and their support. Both conversations can be very helpful in Beulah's progress.

Remember to make calls during working hours as often as possible so you talk to a machine, if you just want to leave a message. You can always invite them to a follow-up conversation, if needed.

Making parents part of the learning process, for assistance or to share in the pride of accomplishment, are essential elements to changing lives.

———————

Creating the best environment for learning and setting high and appropriate expectations are skills and activities that come naturally to some educators, and are learned by others. For many teachers it is a combination of the two, but all teachers never stop improving in both areas.

Teachers who emphasize *learning* never lose focus on why they teach. These same teachers have the passion to make positive changes in the lives of their students. And these same teachers will always be cognizant of the importance of expectations and environment.

Setting appropriate expectations and establishing the best learning environment will help change lives.

◆ Be consistent with the rules you use. Be sure to set boundaries and to establish logical consequences but, most important, be consistent in what you do with the consequences.

◆ If you have an American Flag in your classroom, use it. Recite the Pledge of Allegiance first thing in the morning, even if the rest of the school doesn't. (And if they don't, find out why.) Then, every time you make a reference to freedom, to being an American, democracy, or related topics, point out the flag. Encourage pride in being an American every chance you have.

◆ Look at your desk, your grade book, your plan book, your room, and your general organizational structure. Then ask yourself, "If I was unable to finish the day, could a substitute walk in here and take over?"

◆ Create "teaching moments." For example, if you have an unscheduled fire drill, when the kids return, ask them questions like: "What would you have done if the fire alarm went off during recess?" "What would you do if you saw someone whose clothes were on fire?" "Name three things you should look for in your own house that could cause a fire (overloaded plugs, oily rags in a pile, letters or newspapers near a candle or stove, etc.). Look for ways to make *anything and everything* a teaching moment.

◆ Emphasize over and again that education is important. Give examples as often as you can about how someone reached a goal or made a difference because they were educated. Find ways to share the importance of what kids are studying.

◆ Let them know what you expect. We all want to know what a job involves and why we are doing it. Expectations are easier to achieve if clearly communicated, understood, and meaningful.

◆ Use rewards to accomplish goals. Some examples?

- For handing in homework on time all week, we play kickball for 15 minutes on the last day of the week.
- Use extra field trips for rewards.
- Every Friday we play Jeopardy to reinforce major concepts studied during the week. Divide the class into two teams and the teams compete for a prize— and they learn in the process.

- No weekend assignment for everyone who earns an A or B on this quiz. (For those that don't, the weekend assignment consists of work related to the quiz so that they will do better on Monday!)

◆ Monitor your student's progress or lack of it, and keep them informed of what they need to do if they're having problems. Equally as important is to tell students what they're doing right. Short written notes that praise success with academics or success in outside activities will tell the student that you care. Nothing breeds more success than a sincere and unexpected compliment. Nothing promotes success more than encouraging those having problems.

◆ Know the state or local standards for the subject you are teaching; better yet, have the kids know them. Tell the kids that when they are doing an assignment and it addresses one of the standards, if they put the appropriate standards identification number on the paper, you will give them bonus points. It will keep them thinking about the standards and help them develop ownership.

◆ One school I know of has an "adopt-a-standard" program for each grading period. This is done through subject areas or departments. They laminate a selected written standard and post it in appropriate classrooms. In addition, they give each student and parent a copy. They focus on academic improvements on that standard. It helps focus attention and effort on the importance of the standards.

◆ Move around the classroom frequently. You are able to keep track of what students are accomplishing or not accomplishing. It keeps kids on their toes, and the entire classroom climate will improve.

◆ Don't let students crowd around your desk. You can't see what's happening in the room.

◆ Offer choices to the students in determining assignments, within boundaries. Remember, it is better to have a low-motivated student write a paper on anything than to have that person do nothing. More examples?

- The history of rock and roll is history,
- an essay comparing and contrasting modern clothing styles is a comparative essay,
- a speech promoting the right of boys to wear earrings in school is a persuasive speech,
- the biology of cosmetics is still science,
- the mathematics of the stock market or the odds of gambling are mathematics, and
- the physics of the operation of a 283-cubic-inch Chevy engine is still physics.

◆ Have a student of the day, student of the month, family of the week, best class attendance award, best good deed, or most friendly award. Use photos of students and utilize the newspaper. Teachers who come up with strange awards that are fun yet meaningful and appropriate can make a difference for the morale and attitude of their students.

◆ Know exactly, to the last detail, what you are doing during every lesson. Expect trouble if you are unprepared. Teaching well prepared is a hundred times easier than when you wing it. Kids deserve well-planned lessons.

◆ Use videos to promote thinking and discussion. Stop a video at planned times and ask specific questions about what they have just watched. This will either solidify the content of the video or encourage divergent thinking. They will also pay better attention if they expect a discussion (or short quiz) after every fifteen minutes or so. This works and is a great tool for learning.

◆ Pair low-motivated students with highly-motivated students and work in groups. Use the concept of student teams to learn. Evaluate using a group grade rather than an individual grade at times. This type of teaching promotes cooperative learning skills.

◆ Make sure that your classroom rules, rewards, and consequences are understood, supported, and accepted by all segments of the school organization, including the administration, fellow teachers, support staff, and especially the students. Your system may seem too easy, too tough, or too strange if others don't understand your rationale.

◆ Display your diplomas. Be proud of them. It tells a kid that you had to earn an education to provide one. It also promotes questions about attending college, etc.

◆ Have a lot of big green plants in your classroom. They make the place nicer, the air cleaner, and they add a touch of home.

◆ New teachers have been told to "never smile before Christmas!" Bah, humbug! Smile immediately and don't stop. Discipline is built on respect, not fear.

◆ If there is a behavior problem, move closer to the offender. Proximity makes a difference. In many cases, the problem will simply stop because you are close. And many times you won't have to interrupt your teaching to make the correction!

◆ Again, *be consistent!* Consistency rules in discipline, expectations, neatness, and procedures. Kids want consistency as long as it makes sense and is fair.

◆ Never discipline when you are angry. If you are mad, settle down and wait before you proceed. Put the kid in a holding situation until you can respond with dignity and patience. This same concept works well at your house too.

◆ Never make a threat you're not willing to carry out. Particularly, never make a stupid threat. For example, don't say, "The next time I mark your name on the board for an inappropriate behavior you will be sent to Siberia" because when his name *is* written on the board, you must at least send him to the airport. If you say it, you must do it! It's best never to threaten at all, just share honest consequences.

◆ All communications should be based on honest information presented in a tactful way that is respectful of the receiver. Don't be afraid to admit you don't have all the answers, but always seek to find them. And never fail to apologize when you make an error in information or judgment.

◆ If the phone rings in your room, demonstrate manners by excusing yourself and then, if you can, ask the person to call back later and let the kids hear you say "We are in the middle of an important lesson." Much will be learned by the way you demonstrate simple acts of courtesy and behavior, as well as by the way you share the importance of the learning process.

◆ Make it clear what you want kids to learn, what the lesson is about, and what your expectations are. A simple statement during the lesson covering these three items can greatly promote learning.

"No horse gets anywhere
until he is harnessed.

No steam of gas drives
anything until it is confined.

No Niagara is ever turned into light
and power until it is
tunneled.

No life ever grows great until it is
focused, dedicated,
disciplined."

Charles F. Kettering
1876-1958

Chapter Eleven

The Fun Police

Let's talk about fun—but let's define it first.

When I think of fun, I think of enjoyment. "That was a fun night," doesn't have to mean you laughed yourself to the point of incontinence. "Our minister is a fun person" can mean that he or she has a sense of humor, recognizes enjoyable situations, is positive, and smiles a lot. (It can also mean they enjoy the Three Stooges or a good laugh, as my minister does!) Or "fun" can mean being satisfied, peaceful, and without stress.

In this chapter, let's agree that "fun" is synonymous with an enjoyable or good experience. I also think that fun should be a defining term of your job.

I suspect that my students rate me as a fun teacher because I tell stories and jokes, insert humor, and find the positive side of most issues. (Remember, my blood type is B-Positive!) I've also discovered that most people enjoy situations when they experience success and are happy.

Many teachers whom I consider exceptionally talented are not necessarily funny but their classes are places of true success and real learning. They are positive life changers. So, one can be fun without being funny, successful without being a standup comic, and a life changer without shtick.

I truly believe fun is essential to learning. I used to cringe when I would hear a kid tell his/her parents that my classes were funny. I didn't want Mom or Dad to think that being funny was the goal, so I would often quickly ask, "Did you learn anything?" I did this so parents understood that learning was more important to me than entertaining. It was, however, a great compliment when kids said my class was fun and we learned a lot, because "learning a lot" was always the goal.

What do I mean about being the "Fun Police"? This sounds like some sort of program, weird game, or even military adventure. None of the above. Let me describe it through a story—actually two. They are revised versions of real tales, modified only a bit to honor the privacy of those involved. The stories parallel each other and really drive home, to me, the need for the Fun Police.

When I was just a young pup I taught part of the day and also served as the building principal, coach, and student council sponsor, plus attended graduate school and was a husband and father of two young girls. Fortunately, I also worked with some of the most dedicated and outstanding teachers one could meet. (More about them in the chapter to follow.)

One such person was a primary grade teacher who was almost three times older than me, and certainly far wiser. She was an exceptional teacher.

Almost every day we were the last two to leave the building. Even the janitor was done before we left. I was usually doing office work after practice and she didn't believe in taking work home, so she stayed until all papers were graded, the bulletin boards updated, the next day's lesson plans were completed, notes were written for kids, the reward dish was checked and refilled, and the creative things planned for the next day were unpacked and ready to fly. Her room was a maze of excitement and learning, and she was just simply amazing herself.

Almost every night when she left she would call out to me, "Good night, Jim. Kiss your babies for me." My babies included my wife and two kids. I yelled a response back and sometimes I could hear her laughing as the main doors to the building clicked behind her. We had a very special relationship. She could easily have been my grandmother. She knew more about teaching than I knew about life in total. It was ironic that I was her evaluator when in fact she taught me more than many educators I ever met.

She also kidded with me, and I gave her a hard time, which she loved. She often told me that I needed a good spanking and would poke me in the arm and call me a young whippersnapper, a term we seldom hear these days. I'm not sure I even know what it means!

On a certain Monday, well into the school year, I heard the front door click about six o'clock and looked out my office window to see this lady, who I will call Madge, walking toward her car. Funny, I thought, she didn't say goodbye.

The next day, on one of my normal rounds of the classrooms to say hello to kids and teachers, I noticed Madge was hard at work promoting her own special version of learning and magic.

That night, again around six, the door clicked. Madge had left again without a word. This was certainly not like her and I couldn't think of any reason why she would break tradition two nights in a row. So I jotted a note to see her on Wednesday. As it turned out, I was able to watch her teach for a few minutes as I visited the classrooms. As always she was right on target; in fact, I wished I could have taped her for every young teacher to see.

Wednesday night I heard her close her classroom door and start walking down the halls a little before six. I called out to her, "Good night, Madge. See you tomorrow." She responded with dim enthusiasm, "Good night, Jim." At this point I recognized that something was not right.

The next day I checked on her again. Everything seemed okay. She was a good teacher, and maybe a better actress. That night I decided I would meet her on the way out if she failed to say anything to me.

She didn't say anything when it was time to leave. I met her just as she was about to exit the building. Our conversation went something like this….

"Good night, Madge."

"Good night, Jim."

"Is everything okay, Madge?"

"Everything is fine," she replied sternly.

"Are you sure?"

"I said (pause) everything is fine," she replied with some agitation.

"Well, if that's the case, would you do me a favor? Would you go down to the bathroom, look into the mirror, and tell your face? Because you don't look like everything is fine," I said with a chuckle.

She didn't find my wise crack funny. Then she began to sob. Not cry, just sob. I told her to follow me. We went back into her classroom, sat down in the ridiculously low chairs, and I asked her again what was wrong.

In an emotion-packed session she told me that her husband had left her on Sunday. She had no idea where he was. They had been married nearly 50 years. My first thought was that her husband was kind of old and he may just be lost and wandering around their large yard. Fortunately, I kept the thought to myself. Instead, I asked what steps she had taken to solve the problem, though, in my heart, I suspected she hadn't done anything at all. I asked her what her daughters thought of the situation (hoping she had told them, and fearful she hadn't.) She said she was so embarrassed she had not called them. I then asked what her minister had said, knowing how involved they were in the church. She hadn't told him either. She finally admitted that I was the first to know.

I told Madge that after she got home I would call her and that I would either come to pick her up and take her to our house for dinner or I would come over to her house to help her sort things out. I told her that she needed to call her kids and/or minister, and that she was not to return to work until she handled this situation. I emphasized that family comes first always, and in all ways. She reminded me that (due to other circumstances) she had no remaining sick days and needed every day to make her retirement quota. I told her that she would not be charged for any days missed even if I had to pay for the sub myself, and that was guaranteed. She settled down, gained her composure, and went home.

I called her 30 minutes later from my own home. She had already called her daughters and the minister and they were all going to meet that night. She thanked me, and I told her I would have a sub in place for her tomorrow and to call me if I could help.

A while later she called to report that her husband was at his brother's farm in a neighboring state, he was well but confused. It seems he had an episode of some sort and just took off. This was years before we knew much about Alzheimer's and other forms of dementia. The next morning, about seven, Madge walked into my office. She was there to work. I called off the sub and Madge and I sat and talked for a few minutes. She cried again and told me that the daughters went out to get their dad and bring the car home. They had a lot of things to think out, but Madge said she needed to be at work that day. She also said that she didn't know what would have happened had I not questioned her in the hallway. She was desperate, despondent, humiliated, and grateful that I cared enough to notice that something was wrong.

At that moment a light bulb went off in my head. It dawned on me that for many of the people who work at the school, this place is their only family away from home. That many of the people here share problems, concerns, and issues with peers that they may never share at home. That work offered a place for them to release and to grow and solve problems. It also came to light that it was every employee's responsibility to insure, or at least check, on the well-being, or "fun factor," of everyone else. That the health of the system was no better than the health of the people who worked there. That if we didn't care about each other at the schoolhouse, maybe in some circumstances no one cared.

Years later, after I had moved to another district, one of the teachers I knew committed suicide. She didn't show up for work one snowy, cold, blistery winter day. The superintendent couldn't reach her on the phone and it was not like her to miss or be late without calling. She would never abandon her kids. After a while, the police went to her home and found her body. What they discovered did not fit what people knew, or thought, about her. I often wondered if there had been a better "Fun Police" concept in her school, might she still be alive today? Did anyone sense a problem? Did she feel comfortable enough to share her concerns with anyone at the school? Maybe not. Maybe this was an unusual situation. I'll always wonder. She taught two of my kids, and she facilitated learning in an exceptional way. It was a terrible loss.

The Fun Police is a squad of caring individuals who look out for each other. They sense when someone is not having "fun" at work and seek to find out why. Maybe, as in the case of Madge, all it takes is a simple question. Maybe just letting someone know that they don't seem the same, that they appear to be down, discouraged, or lack the passion and happiness they usually demonstrate, is enough.

There are some categories of co-workers who will always need the attention of the Fun Police. How about new teachers who may also be new to the community? These folks, either single or married, may have few friends, if any. How nice would it be to invite them to go shopping, come to your place for dinner, attend church with you, or just to have coffee with after work?

What about the family having its first baby? Usually these are kids going through the changes and pressures of parenthood. Wouldn't a visit from the Fun Police be wonderful?

And of course we all know the needs of the teacher or employee who has a spouse with cancer, a recent death of a family member, a sick child, or a parent they need to put in a nursing home, an addict in the household, or a kid in and out of jail. The list is endless and the support that we can offer them is immense.

Is this in your job description? Did you learn about this added responsibility of the Fun Police at the university? Have you ever attended a professional development seminar on serving the needs of your co-workers? The answer to all of these questions is probably no. What a shame. Because if we are to change lives, who says they should be student lives only? If we are to be professionally trained to infiltrate the mind, assess needs, provide direction and instruction, and make a difference, why can't we expand that expertise to everyone in the schoolhouse? Why can't we care for and love the teacher next door, the custodian, the secretary, and yes, even the administrator? We can, and we should.

Teachers Change Lives 24/7

And the Fun Police should not just be a silent squad of problem seekers and solvers. They should also be an active squad of fun seekers and spirit builders! The Fun Police should be finding ways of congratulating and supporting the good things going on, whether personal or educational, private or public, a new hairdo or an *Award of Excellence.* The Fun Police should be ready to give a pat on the back, send a flower, mail a card, make an announcement, shake a hand, initiate a conversation.

Imagine how positive the climate of the school building or school system would be if everyone spent as much time caring for each other as many do complaining about each other. What if every new or struggling teacher felt the support of a caring faculty? What if a veteran teacher who witnessed another teacher struggling with achievement scores, discipline, or motivation, quietly offered some help without feeling like they were intruding? What if principals and parking lot monitors alike felt like they worked for a system that truly, really, honestly cared not just about the students but also about the employees?

Is the concept of the Fun Police far-fetched and so idealistic that it is just a bunch of verbal hooey? I really don't think so. I also think that a Fun Police Force of one is better than no Force at all. I also think that when faculties talk about this unwritten part of their job, and when administrators encourage this type of activity, and when association presidents support this concept, it takes on a life of its own and becomes more real than imaginary.

It boils down to this. You see a problem and address it. You sense a concern and you offer help. You witness something special, new, different, or positive, and you celebrate it. You may not really like Stacey's new hairdo, but she hasn't had one in 30 years and it is a step in the right direction—you tell her she looks great, and she feels good. You sense that George is thinner and you tell him he looks like he has dropped a few pounds and looks super. You just made his day. When Marvin comes to work sour and void of his usual spunk, you ask him if he is okay? When he sadly says yes, you ask him again. And if you don't believe him, you remind him that you are available if he ever needs anything at any time.

You know what the Fun Police can do? They can create a caring workplace with healthy, happy, motivated people who *can do their jobs better for kids*. They can, and will, make the schoolhouse a better place for learning. They can and will make their own house a better place for living. Everyone wins.

Why not be the first member of the Fun Police at your school?

◆ If you see something you like about a person, share it. Don't waste a compliment. It is one thing to say to yourself, "My, he looks nice today," but imagine how much better it would be to tell the person!

◆ Have dress-up days as opposed to dress-down days. Studies show that when students "dress-up" it fosters a better self-image, higher self-esteem, and better behavior.

◆ When a fellow staff member is honored for something, never, never, never criticize anything about the honor. Be the first to congratulate them. And, if you cannot say anything positive, say nothing.

◆ If your room is clean and neat every day, thank your custodian. Then tell your principal what a great job the custodian is doing.

◆ If you want parents to be on your side, be on theirs. When a parent comes to complain about something, *don't get defensive*. First try to wear their moccasins. Listen, restate, and then try to come to a mutual understanding of the problem. It takes practice and tact to manage conflict, but *most* of the time you can do it if you just back away and try to see the situation from their point of view. Then slowly, carefully bring them around to hear your point of view.

◆ If a kid burps or toots or does something else that causes the class to laugh, seize the moment and laugh with him, and then move to the next item of business. Later, privately, ask the student to try not to do that again. Don't make a big deal out of it. Be human. Sometimes it *is* funny. If a kid makes a habit of the situation, or does it on purpose to disrupt the class, that's a different situation. Even then handle it privately.

◆ The next time you get a new textbook series that you feel is working exceptionally well and meeting the goals of your program, go and tell someone. We often hear about what doesn't work in schools, but how cool is it to hear about what works well! Maybe even consider writing an article for the paper, giving a note to the principal, crafting a thank you to the Curriculum Committee chairman, or providing an insert in the next school newsletter. Share success and watch good things happen!

◆ Send birthday cards to your peers and students. You will never know the benefits of this simple act. They don't have to be expensive cards to make the point. A short, sincere written note in the card increases the value by 237% (Research provided by best guess).

◆ Develop strong teaching skills. T.E.S.A., Keys to Motivation, P.R.I.D.E., T.E.A.C.H., and similar programs that promote better teaching skills are great for all teachers, no matter how experienced or confident you are. These types of programs, when offered to your staff at your school, can change the entire climate of learning.

◆ When someone interrupts your class in person or via the intercom, always demonstrate polite and respectful behavior. Even if the disruption causes you personal constipation, don't let on to the kids. How you respond will be mirrored by how they respond in the future. It even helps to repeat the announcement or to make a positive comment about the announcer or subject.

◆ Treat your work colleagues at every level with respect and compassion. What you give is what you will get. I remember a certain grade school teacher whose room was always spotless and to whom the janitor provided "above-and-beyond" service. Why? She asked the janitor what she could do to make his job easier. He asked her if she could have the kids put their chairs on their desks before they left, he would have enough extra time to wash her boards every night. She not only complied, but she asked the kids to pick up any loose paper around their desk as well. She did more and thus he did more. She also made him fudge for Christmas. Simple courtesy to each other yielded greater service and appreciation.

◆ When things get you down, look up.

◆ Be aware of the mental and emotional health of your fellow staff members. If they seem depressed, angry, or are behaving in an unusual way, ask if they are okay. They may only need someone to talk to, or to know that someone cares. Be that someone. Watch out for others.

◆ Play academic games and have tournaments as a way to review materials. In-the-room baseball is a fun way to review through team play. How do you play? Divide the class into two teams. Ask the kids questions. Correct answers are hits, wrong answers are outs, or draw a slip that gives other alternatives such as an incorrect answer is a double play, a correct answer is a home run, etc. Kids actually get up and move to corners of the rooms that serve as bases. If a kid gets stumped, have a limited number of pinch hitters for each team (a pinch hitter is when the entire team can confer on the answer). This is a fun way to review material.

◆ When making a presentation, use humor, inspiration, and emotion to involve your students, staff, and audience. Practice this art and don't give up when you mess up; everyone messes up once in a while when presenting.

◆ Suggest that your district offer incentives for teachers to take "teacher effectiveness" programs. If they can't offer money, have them consider other incentives like release time, extra teaching supplies, or hours toward in-house college credits.

◆ Don't be afraid to ask for help. If you are having problems with a lesson, a kid, an administrator, at home, with your car, with anything, just ask for help. After you get it, send a thank you note, a flower, or a card. Each act of helping and thanking builds a better learning community.

Chapter Twelve

A Cast of Characters

This is a chapter about real people who have been—many still are—making a difference for kids.

There was such a huge pool to pick from but, sadly, I can only select a few to share with you. I have already introduced Mr. Ruggles and Mr. B. And you've met others as you journeyed this far, like Dr. Ben and Madge.

I want to share what I learned from an additional handful of characters. If I could choose (with one exception), these are the people I would want my own kids (now my grandkids) to have as teachers. They came up through the ranks, got better from taking risks, learned from professional development, and demonstrated a real passion for the profession. They have made teaching better because each of them has always been willing to share what they know with others. And because, whether they knew it or not, they were proud badge bearers of the Fun Police.

Mike Klippert started teaching one semester after I did. Before Mike's arrival, I was the only male in my building. Being the only male had advantages like a private bathroom, being the exclusive recipient of "motherly advice," and never being asked to bring food to the teacher's workroom. But a male partner also helped share some of the responsibilities, like having a back-up for physical ed, someone to talk sports with, someone to help me remodel the archaic science lab I inherited, and someone with whom to build a personal friendship. We were both young married guys. Mike and his wife had two little boys. We had two little girls. Both families grew up together. Years later a third boy was added to his family, and the first boy joined ours. Mike and his wife and Barb and I took Lamaze classes together. It was the first time that either Mike or I would go into the delivery room. We both survived the class and the deliveries!

We have moved apart and our families don't get together as often as they should, but we are both still married to the same wives and both still working in education. As I write this book, Mike is still teaching, and I work with schools as a speaker and consultant. The passion of teaching that we experienced during our first years together has never faded.

Why is Mike listed in my Cast of Characters? Well, I could say that his being a nationally recognized Milken Foundation Scholar would be reason enough, but Mike would cringe at that. He is a private, quiet man who doesn't like to talk in front of groups, wants no personal attention, and accepted this well-deserved honor with immense humility. But that is the Mike Klippert you would see, not the Mike behind the doors of a classroom. He certainly won't like being on these pages, but he needs to be here.

He exemplifies teaching at its best. The two of us, over the years, played countless practical jokes on each other, often involving our students and the faculty. Everyone knew we were best of friends, had a lot of fun together, and enjoyed a good laugh.

We sponsored field trips together. We took kids roller skating, sledding, to museums and baseball games, almost everywhere. Lots of parents left our wee rural community for the big city of Chicago for the very first time because of the trips Mike and I planned and executed. We delighted in expanding the horizons of both our students and their families.

I especially remember the time when we took a busload to Chicago and part of the adventure was to see the Windy City from the observatory of the John Hancock Building. One of the eighth-grade boys went a little goofy on us when we took the express elevator to reach the observatory level. He wouldn't take the elevator back down. Mike single-handedly took charge of the entire group while I walked down *ninety-plus floors* with this little guy. When we met at the bus, the little guy jumped inside as happy as he could be. (They almost needed paramedics to haul my sorry carcass in the doors.) No one could understand why, later, the two of us laughed so hard and for so long.

Mike is in my cast of characters for a couple of reasons in particular. He was (and is) an outstanding teacher. He has taught the hormonally challenged (seventh and eighth graders) from his first day until the present. He is definitely a member of the Fun Police. He knows each and every student, not just by name but by their academic record, their needs, their home situation, and their abilities. Without them knowing it, he customizes his teaching and expectations to fit them as individuals. No teacher I have known works harder to meet the needs of every child. He does it without seeking praise or recognition. He does it because they deserve it.

His lessons are well planned and yet spontaneous when it fits. He encourages kids to get involved and always uses a variety of teaching methods. He has always presented and crafted alternative teaching opportunities. I can't imagine a day going by when Mike doesn't have a one-on-one pep talk with a student; when he doesn't verbally, or in writing, give a kid a much-needed compliment, or when he doesn't challenge a kid to do better.

I moved from being his teaching partner to becoming the principal of the building *and* his teaching partner, and then became the superintendent and high school principal, and finally, after a consolidation with another district, the superintendent. Never once did I deal with a discipline problem coming from Mike Klippert's class. Never once did I hear a parental complaint about his teaching, grading, or procedures. Never once did I witness, or even consider, anything negative about Mike Klippert the teacher. Why? He disciplined the best way, *by not needing to*. He kept his students involved, engaged, excited, happy, and interested. His classes were full of things to do, and his kids responded by learning. Those kids scored well, grew up well, and knew they had a confidant and friend as well as a teacher.

The other reason Mike Klippert is included in this chapter, if another reason is needed, is because he was a schoolhouse friend. He helped me, listened to me, and shared with me. We would talk teaching, talk kids, and share teaching strategies. We mentored to each other without knowing it. When either of us had issues at home, we had each other at school. When we had a kid with a special need, we both worked on the kid, and shared the need with other teachers. When I needed an ear, hand, heart, head, mind, laugh, spark, or shoulder, Mike provided one. No questions asked. He made me a better teacher and that helped me change lives, 24/7. Every teacher needs a Mike Klippert. Every teacher needs to be a Mike Klippert. Milken Scholar? You bet. Life changer? 24/7.

Greg Hopton taught fifth grade. There are many things I could share about his teaching, but a couple jump out as very special. I know that students remember the year they spent with him because he made his passion for the outdoors come alive. Greg planned and implemented outstanding experiences for kids that reflected his love of wildlife, the outdoors, and nature. He took advantage of an area a few miles from the district where eagles nested. He planned numerous adventures where kids experienced what he taught. He was always willing to share this excitement with other teachers at other grades.

Greg also taught manners. He used to have his students set a dinner table and he taught, demonstrated, and had kids experience situations where all sorts of manners were needed. Even his "rules" were centered on appropriate manners. He once told me that this was a critical time for many kids. Some, as we all know, come from environments where proper manners are not expected or displayed. Some kids just don't hear a "third party" talk about the importance of good manners. Greg used to weave the teaching of manners throughout his lesson plans. Can you think of a better life-long skill to teach kids than proper manners? Greg Hopton changed lots of lives by sharing his own principles and passions.

If you have a passion for something that you can share in your lessons, why not do it? I have a very good friend who taught junior high science. He too is an avid outdoorsman and very interested in astronomy. He would offer optional star gazing opportunities for kids and their parents on clear (and often cold) nights from various spots out in the country. Parents and students would flock to these adventures and share the excitement of something he truly loved to do.

Everyone wins when this happens.

Meet Brad Albrecht. This gentleman continues to change lives in many ways. Recently my daughter-in-law Vanessa told me that she used to love a certain teacher because she focused on skill rather than talent. I asked her to explain this, and she very articulately said that people are born with talent, but develop skill. Her take was that many coaches and teachers want to work with kids that have talent and often favor them over kids with less natural ability who need more skill development.

Her hypothesis is easy to understand. What coach, art teacher, or choral director doesn't relish the chance to work with someone with a natural ability to throw, draw, or sing? Someone who needs refinement of skills rather than basic skill development? Vanessa told me that some of the teachers she had were more skill oriented and demonstrated a high interest in teaching kids who needed skill development at least as much (if not more) than time spent with the natural achiever. Her feeling was that sometimes this type of teaching demonstrated a greater personal interest in the students, was a big motivator, and really made all students feel valued and important. Good points from a good thinker.

As she was talking I was thinking of one person who fit the description perfectly. Brad Albrecht. I first met Brad in my early years as a teacher. He came to the district as a physical education, health, driver's education, coaching combo. He was young, single, good looking, a hometown boy, a natural athlete, and his parents were established in the community and well respected. Brad and I hit it off early since both of us found ourselves supplementing our incomes by working for the district during summer and winter vacations as maintenance men. In fact, over the years, the two of us painted every wall in the entire district at least once—including many of the outside walls as well! We could paint, fix, install lockers, and often looked like Oliver and Hardy in the process. (If you don't know who Oliver and Hardy are you are missing some quality entertainment!)

Brad became a member of the Illinois High School Basketball Coaches Hall of Fame with a lifetime record of 541-

291. He accomplished this goal not because our town was blessed with horizontally-enhanced super stars but because he knew how to do two things very well. Brad was a master at confidence building and skill development. Amazing, but these two concepts are fundamental to teaching success at any grade level, any subject, at any school, under any circumstances.

He could take a mediocre basketball player, one who was not blessed with exceptional talent, and turn him into a fine athlete. He did it by employing all the skills of an exceptional educator. He knew the person. He worked hard at knowing the student's background, opportunities, and needs. If a kid needed to work on the farm to help the family, Brad cut him some slack to be on the team and help with the family needs. If a kid was struggling with academics (but trying hard), Brad made sure help was available, and gave the student opportunities to achieve both academically and athletically. Brad never forgot the order of importance of these two either. If a kid got into trouble, Brad listened, adapted, and supported the student, as long as the student was on the right track. He didn't break rules or give one student an advantage over another. He didn't give kids a "pass" at practice, but he might alter the schedule to meet the student's needs. Brad followed the rules, but sometimes reshaped them, within acceptable parameters, to best allow a student to learn.

Brad Albrecht applied the same ideals and concepts in the academic classes he taught. He also crafted individual educational plans for any student, at any level, for any need, long before special ed ever trademarked the term. Brad was strict, but fair. He set high expectations, but realistic ones for the student. He followed the rules, but when the rules didn't fit, he wasn't afraid to debate an alternative. Brad never thought twice about getting a parent involved if he thought it would help, and never thought twice about taking a parent to task if he thought they weren't helping. He taught and led with conviction and courage. He changed lives every day. He still does. Brad was the kind of leader I encouraged to become an administrator so he could lead teachers as well as students. He dragged his feet for years, in my opinion, because he didn't want to stop teaching and coaching. To students, he was always "Coach." A well-deserved title because Brad was more than a teacher, he was a coach to everyone, always providing motivation, skill development, and opportunities.

Finally he became a principal and soon rose to the rank of superintendent. I recently visited Brad at the pre-K to 12 district he leads. He is well respected by teachers and the community. A couple of things really impressed me as he took me on a tour of the district, the same one where I taught, became a principal, and was superintendent. First, a great many, if not a majority, of the teachers I met were former students of Brad's. They respected him so much they came back to teach for him. Second, as we walked through the building, kids from all age groups greeted him. He had a story about most of them. He knew kids in lower elementary grades all the way to high school seniors.

I witnessed an obvious bond between the students and their superintendent. He knew them all. And he told me how the district was adapting to their needs. He no longer coaches but the new athletic complex is named in his honor. Brad will always be the "Coach."

Her name will remain changed, to protect the innocent. I will call her Mrs. Breckenridge. She taught me a subject in high school that will also remain nameless. The subject, and her name, is incidental to why she is listed in my Cast of Characters.

Mrs. Breckenridge was one of the worst teachers I ever experienced. No, she was the very worst. I am listing her with some great teachers because she taught me many things *not* to do. She taught me that when you get old, accept it and do it gracefully. Don't try to look 20, 30, or more years younger than you are. Kids really don't care how old you are chronologically as long as you can relate to them and help them learn. Mrs. Breckenridge did all the wrong things to look younger, act younger, and seem "cool." All she accomplished was looking like an old person trying to look younger, act younger, and trying to be "cool." She was far from "cool." She provided us with great fun with her dress and behavior. Yes, I'm sorry to admit it, but we made fun of her behind her back. It happens.

She also flirted. This is a serious mistake for any teacher, at any grade, for any reason. You are the teacher, they are the kids, and that is that. She liked to flirt with the boys in my class, and flirting got you some leeway with grades. If she liked you, she would grade the subjective work in your favor. We knew it, the girls knew it, and as far as I know, no one ever complained about it. They might not have complained because, in general, she was an easy grader. Kids might have feared that any mention of favoritism might cause her to grade normally and, as a result, we would actually get what we deserved in terms of grades.

Her assignments were often silly and seemed to be ones that fit the department's requirements of so many assignments per week, or whatever. Many of them were returned to us long after we handed them in, never discussed, and not used as a learning tool. What a waste of time and opportunity.

And, she was boring. Worse, Boring with a Big "B." I dreaded her class, hated having to "kiss up" to her by making her think she was funny or cute, and despised the fact that I was wasting 45 minutes every day learning practically nothing, or maybe absolutely nothing. And the scariest thing of all was that I don't think she knew how bad she was.

I often wondered, didn't someone know what kind of teacher she was? Didn't her peers, evaluator, supervisor, department chair, or anyone else know? If they did, why didn't they do something about it? In a book I co-authored called *The Perfect School* we devote an entire chapter to this very topic. It is called, "Eliminate the Weakest Link." Miss Breckenridge was just that. I will never forget her, unfortunately.

What did I learn from her? Don't be buddies with your students (or in her case, don't try to be buddies.) Don't flirt or act inappropriately. Don't ever assume that kids aren't judging your actions, your dress, and your mannerisms. Don't give lame assignments and mandatory, no-learn assessments. Grade, return, discuss all tests and assignments and make them valuable parts of the learning program. Everyone is boring at times, but don't be Boring with a capital "B".

When it is time to retire, retire.

Paula Shea teaches kindergarten in a small rural school. I previously mentioned that she has the custodian come into her classroom, in his traditional bib overalls, to help teach her kids the letter "T." Paco, as everyone calls him, brings his toolbox and tool belt and starts to talk about a lot of his tools, taking care to emphasize anything that starts with "T." It is a very special demonstration, one that I had the honor of watching one day.

Paula, you see, is very creative. She also involves as many people in the teaching process as possible. She utilizes alternative teaching spaces, parental help, and goes to extremes to find a program that meets a student's individual needs.

Paula also invented "hips and lips." She merely utters this phrase and her kids know that when they march down the halls of the school they are not to talk (lips) and they must keep their hands to themselves (by their hips). It is a clever way to get a concept across.

When Paula is with her students what you *sense* is love, respect, and order. The kids absolutely love her, and why not? She absolutely loves them. It shows. But she also respects those little guys and demands that they treat each other with respect. She teaches the curriculum very well and her students score very high on assessments; but more than anything, her kids focus on how to do the right thing.

Paula was so passionate about teaching values to her own kids that she was one of the driving forces for development of the district's pre-K to 12 character education program. The program is called V.I.P. for Very Important Principles. It has won many awards and has been adopted by not only the school system but by the five communities it encompasses. She worked tirelessly to get this program started and established. It all began in a kindergarten classroom.

Her principal once told me that Paula Shea always puts the students first and she believes that being respectful and responsible are just as important as learning the numbers and letters. She lives that belief.

Kindergarten teachers are natural-born collectors. They have to be. They have learning stations, teaching containers, bulletin board "stuff" by the tons, instructional supplies, carpet samples, and craft materials, plus cut out, plastic, painted, cardboard, and other varieties of *letters*. It should be a law that kindergarten rooms all have attached storage garages. Paula is no exception, but her room is always orderly, neat, and defined. Even with 20 or so urchins around, and with learning stations, computers, tables, and reading areas occupying needed space, the room is organized and impressive. She is a master at keeping things in place and available and teaches her students this important skill.

Walk into Paula Shea's room and she will introduce you to the kids. You will see her smile and feel the bond she has with those developing wonders. She will make you feel important and make your presence important to the learning process.

What have I learned from Paula Shea? That you can be passionate about what you do at any level. You can be orderly and organized no matter how many tons of "things" line your walls and shelves. You can teach respect and responsibility to not only your own students but to an entire district. And you can come to school everyday and change a life just by doing your best, expecting the best, and sharing your love of learning.

There are a couple of people I need to mention because they both gave me some great tools to use.

One is the famous educator Harry Wong. Any book, tape, lecture, seminar, or article by Harry Wong is worth reading, watching, or attending. He is a wonderful motivator and idea-giver. One of the many ideas I learned from him—probably in writing, on a video, and maybe even at one of his lectures—has to do with record keeping. I used it for years and even added my own little twist. Let me share it with you, giving full credit to Mr. Wong.

Most teachers still use a grade book even though computers are quickly taking over the world of record keeping. I assume at some point you will simply be able to say the kid's name and the score on the assignment or test and verbal recognition programs and record keeping software will do the rest. Until then you may still feel the need to write the scores and information in a grade book. This idea will help streamline the process.

Although I don't personally know any teacher who was institutionalized because of record keeping, knowing how anal many teachers are, it is possible. What I am referring to is the situation when a teacher meticulously enters the student's name and information into the grade book, usually in alphabetical order, and in the type of print one uses when they first start a fresh checkbook ledger. Then on about the 17th day of school there stands the principal at your door first thing in the morning and next to her is, you guessed it, a new student! You panic, you freak, you picture your grade book with the neatly listed student names, beginning with Rosalie Adams and ending with Ronny Zimmerman, and soon to be followed by this creature. You want so badly to ask if the new student's last name, by any chance is Zygoat, but you hold back. When you find out her name is Sasha McFarland you almost choke.

Okay, I'm being ridiculous—or am I? Anyway, if you use the Harry Wong method you would not be upset at all. You would welcome the new student with open arms knowing that your students have a number as well as a name. The number simplifies bookkeeping, and actually improves it. You introduce yourself to Sasha, introduce her to the class, and have everyone introduce himself or herself to her. Then you proudly tell Sasha that she is number 32.

Here is how the numbers work. When students turn in their papers they put their name in the upper right hand corner, just like students have since paper was invented. But your students also put their number in the upper left hand corner. When papers are collected, someone is asked to put them in numerical order, then double check to make sure they are correctly arranged. The person you select is someone who will not suffer from missing a minute or two of class instruction or individual practice, and someone you can count on. I always made it a habit of not selecting workers or volunteers that needed instruction or practice time to do these kinds of things.

When you get the stack of papers it becomes very easy to enter them in your grade book, or on your computer, if it too is organized numerically. In fact, you can watch ER and never miss a squirt of blood while you accurately enter scores in your grade book.

I added something to the Harry Wong method. In an effort to make as much of the work kids do meaningful, I added a learning component to the number posting. In the upper left hand corner of the main chalk (or white, green, black, electronic) board, I had a box that contained "number directions." I told the students that they needed to watch this box and they had 24 hours from the time a change was posted to follow the directions. The idea was that they would post their number following the directions. For instance, the box might say " ¾ inches high." That meant the number on the top of their papers had to be ¾ inches high. It might say, "written in German." That meant they would write out their number in the German language. Maybe it would direct them to "use Roman numerals," or "enclose your number with a pentagon." I had dozens of options that expanded what they knew and made them learn something interesting, creative, and new. Remember, they had 24 hours, so if they messed up the assignment, they had a day to get it right. It became a learning game—a fun one to boot.

The numbers helped me organize and keep records better and quicker. The number assignment made something that could be purely mundane both fun and educational.

Another person who taught me some neat stuff is author Rick Morris. He has a lot of resources for teachers and the one that I liked most taught about cards. In a nutshell, it went like this. Get a cheap deck of cards. Write each student's name on a card, one card per student. Write the name large and with magic marker. Rick shares various ways to use the cards to call on kids. I would pull out the deck, shuffle them, and call on the top card when doing a question answering session. The kids knew they would be called on sooner or later and raising hands wasn't necessary. The process is totally fair. It also guaranteed that kids would be called on equally. What a clever and useful idea. It took some pressure off the kids, but it kept them attentive. You can even use the deck of cards to randomly select teams for review games. Any teacher can quickly come up with lots of ways to use the cards.

I also used the cards that had already been pulled as support for kids struggling to answer a question. For instance, if I had already called on 10 kids, those 10 kids might think the pressure was off. So, if any student was having a hard time answering a question I drew a card from "used" pile to become a support person who would go over and help the student who was having trouble. No one was then exempt from paying attention. It put an interesting twist on classroom involvement.

You can learn lots of things from folks willing to share and from well-known educational experts. Harry and Rick are just two of countless examples.

Finally, I want to end with an unusual suspect in my Cast of Characters. Her name is Jeanie Probst. She is a Nationally Certified Teacher; in fact, she was one of the "Terrific Ten" in my last district.

At one point in our efforts to create a second-to-none, award-winning district (that operated on a shoestring), we decided to build on something we already knew. We had, over the years, employed a stellar group of teachers. We had eliminated many weak links, added some excellent staff, and retained teachers of the highest quality. How could we utilize this information in a way that would *enhance learning* and make teachers want to continually improve?

We decided to actively engage in the National Board for Professional Teaching Standards program. We had read and heard about this nationwide program that trains and recognizes the best teachers and teaching practices. We dove into the program headfirst. The Board of Education supported the efforts and so did the teachers' association. I could write a chapter on the process and its benefits but let me cut to the chase. We had about 200 teachers in our district then. Ten decided to submit to the program. The work involved is immense. Some say it is more work than earning another degree. Many of my teachers put in well over 400 hours of study and preparation. The statistics for successfully completing the program at that time were discouraging. Many teachers dropped out and many did not receive certification, even at the end of the three-year approval window. Only a small percentage of those enrolled were usually certified at the end of the first year, which is the earliest a person can complete all phases of the process.

We beat all the odds. Ten of our ten were named as National Board Certified Teachers after the first round of assessments and submissions. We dubbed them "The Terrific Ten." We had been told that we may have been the only school to accomplish this feat, certainly in Illinois, maybe in the United States.

This achievement sparked a wave of interest in professional development and the Terrific Ten became ambassadors of the teaching strategies they learned. Not only did they share their expertise, *other teachers were eager to receive it!* Soon there was a list of teachers who wanted to engage in the process, and to this date, every year a new "class" of teachers joins the rank. The goal is to have 25% of the entire district's teaching staff Nationally Certified.

One of the standout leaders in the process was a teacher named Jeanie Probst. Jeanie was a high school math teacher at the time. After she earned her National Board Certification, she became an NBC instructor, and eventually headed the NBC program at her district. Her passion to help other teachers do the best they can, and be the best they can, is almost measureless.

I had listed Jeanie on my Cast of Characters when I first started to outline this chapter. She, like the others, is an inspiration for all students and teachers. But it was a discussion with my son that really confirmed my decision to include Jeanie.

We were talking about this book and about education in general. I asked him, and his wife, to name the teachers that influenced them the most in their lives. Doug named three, and Jeanie Probst was one of them. It was kind of a surprise to me since math was not his favorite subject. So we had this long discussion on the qualities of teachers that make a difference. Let me share how he described Jeanie.

He said that she was a teacher that truly cared if you learned the material. She went the extra step to make sure you understood what was being taught. She facilitated the learning process. Sounds like me talking, doesn't it? But those are his words.

Doug also said that he said he didn't care for her the first semester. She was not entertaining, didn't really teach "out of the box," and was overly professional. She stuck to the topic and was a taskmaster. She was always pleasant and dependable, but she had high expectations and you were to meet them. Those who didn't try in her class were lost in the shuffle. She didn't seem too interested in the kids who couldn't care less but she would bend over backwards if you picked up the pace and got involved. It was up to you. It was an honors course and he said they were treated like honor students. He reported that during the second semester he figured out that she was on his side. She was concerned that everyone learn the subject. She would go to any extent, if you held up your end of the deal. She was fair and she was passionate about teaching. In the long run she may have been the most effective teacher he had.

Doug, my son, had said a lot. He listed the qualities of fairness, setting high expectations, and caring about the learning process as top qualities.

Jeanie Probst continues to educate. She is now a principal and still leads the National Board Certification process. She was one of the best teachers I ever met before she became Nationally Board Certified. By getting involved with NBPTS she demonstrated that she expected as much from herself as she did from her students. She set her own standards very high, and worked hard to achieve them.

Great teachers don't reach one level and stay there; they too continue to learn. *They even change their own lives.*

This is a hard chapter to end. There are so many excellent examples of teachers to learn from. So many that have been willing to share what they know with others, like Harry Wong and Rick Morris. So many who have lead by quiet, unassuming examples, like Mike, Greg, Paula, and Jeanie. And there are a few, a minority, that have taught us what not to do, like Mrs. Breckenridge. I bet you could write your own Cast of Characters as well. I hope you have learned from those you feel were special examples and inspirational in many ways. I hope you also learned from those that were average or below. That is the goal of this chapter, to learn from others. Teachers change lives 24/7. This Cast of Characters includes some of the very best life changers I know.

◆ Consider becoming Nationally Certified. Consider applying for a scholarship or other forms of training or recognition. Talk to your administrator about how you might engage in more professional development opportunities. Demonstrate your willingness to improve. Everyone benefits when a teacher gets better.

◆ The next time someone in the teacher's room criticizes a kid, the principal, the janitor, or anyone, find something positive to say about the person being criticized. Make this a habit. Change the tone.

◆ Send thank you notes to those most often forgotten. How about the art teacher who always helps with every event, the secretary who finds the time to squeeze in extra things for you, the administrator who gets criticized often but most of the time works hard to make your life better, the Board members when they approve a new contract or take some heat for doing what is right, or a dozen other "unsung heroes." Just look around and get writing. Try to write one thank-you note a week to someone who just might need it.

Eat lunch in the school cafeteria. Eat with kids at least once a week.

When the principal or someone else is making an announcement over the intercom, don't in any way make a face or show any other sign of disrespect. Not only is it wrong, but the odds are in favor that it will get back to the person.

One teacher I met simply claps FIVE times in the following way—"clap.....clap......clap, clap, clap"—to get students to calm down. They are taught to join his clapping. By clap number three, they are usually all clapping. They are quiet by the fifth clap. It works.

◆ Use a kitchen timer to keep students on task or to time a certain part of the lesson.

Change the seating chart at least four times a year. Better yet, teach without one. One teacher posts the following rule: "Sit where you like, but if you keep someone from learning, I hope you like where I will seat you."

Never leave a bathroom without checking buttons and zippers and making sure that what is supposed to be tucked in, is. If kids are laughing and you don't know why, check those areas first!

Suggest that the school provide a free lunch to any teacher who eats with the students. (I did it when I was a superintendent and it really promoted the activity.)

Make learning fun and interesting. Let part of you always be like a kid.

◆ Use stories, anecdotes, personal experiences, and mysteries. They will remember the moral to a story long after they have forgotten the class.

◆ Be enthusiastic! They won't be motivated if you aren't. It has to be more than a job for you. Your attitudes, more than anything else, have the greatest impact on the kids. Be motivated yourself!

◆ Use "big space" learning ideas like an outdoor map, a gym-sized ear (with students being the parts of the ear), human spelling (kids representing letters), etc. The possibilities are endless and it makes learning fun.

◆ Use custom-made classroom motivational programs. One teacher uses a "Paw Program." P=Pursue, A=Attack, W=Win. This is posted with some instructions, and they refer to it when they try something new.

◆ At the risk of slight repetition, let me share, in summary, the "Ten Basic Rules You Already Know" that I elaborated upon in *What Every Superintendent and Principal Needs to Know*: (1) Exercise for 30 minutes a day, (2) Don't use any type of tobacco product, (3) Don't drink alcohol [but if you do, do it in considerable and consistent moderation], (4) Eat a balanced diet that contains fruit, vegetables, and whole grains each day, (5) Maintain a healthy weight, (6) Spend time on relationships, (7) Be strong spiritually, (8) Challenge your mind every day, (9) Be proactive, and (10) Wear your seat belt.

"No man will make a great leader who wants to do it all himself, or get all the credit for doing it."

Andrew Carnegie
1835-1919

Chapter Thirteen

What You See is What You Get

There was an ad for Microsoft that ran in many magazines a few years ago. I first saw it in an issue of *National Geographic*. It was a two-page ad that had a teacher standing in front of a line of eight students. I copied one page of the ad (the teacher and four students) and gave Microsoft some free publicity in many of my teacher and administrator workshops. The ad was an exceptional way of demonstrating a point.

Let me create a visual for you if you don't remember or never saw the ad. The teacher is a lady. She is wearing a casual outfit with tennis shoes. She is holding what looks like a clipboard. She is facing a single file line of students. Let me describe the first four in line. The kids, who appear to be 10-12 years old, have on jackets and two are wearing baseball-type caps. The scene is outdoors, maybe next to a museum. You can only see a part of a building behind the teacher and you also see a nicely landscaped sidewalk. Each of the kids appears to be holding a file or clipboard.

The interesting part of this glossy color photograph is the "ghost" lines around the students. Lines that seem to represent what the teacher visualizes. The first student, a young lady, is standing straight, holding her clipboard, and facing the teacher. The "ghost" lines have added a beret to her head and a large artist's paintbrush to one hand. An easel with a sketch of the teacher's face stands in front of the student.

The second student is a young man. He is smiling and appears to be raising his hand ready to ask a question. The ghost lines have added running shorts, an athletic jersey, and a wristband. The smiling boy is clutching an award hanging around his neck and holds, in his uplifted hand, what looks like an Olympic torch.

The third student is standing in line with her notebook open. This young girl's "ghost" lines have added a swimming mask on her head and scuba gear on her back, around her chest, and in her mouth. She appears to have a wet suit on with flippers and she is holding a flashlight.

The final student seems to be of the unisex variety. He or she is standing, facing the teacher, holding the clipboard with both hands and displays a bright smile on his/her face. The "ghost" lines have added a saxophone hanging from his/her neck, and he/she is playing it. Little "ghost" notes are coming out of the instrument.

Four kids standing in line. The expression on the teacher's face is one of pride and ownership. She seems to be saying, "These are my kids. I am proud of them." But the ghost lines tell us even more. The ghost lines define the title of this chapter, *What You See is What You Get*.

One of the most important components of success in anything is having a vision. Business leaders, school administrators, classroom teachers, parents, clergy, anyone who sets goals and works toward meeting them, gets there faster and more effectively if they have vision.

I have a personal example of vision. Shortly after assuming the role of superintendent at the district from which I retired after twelve wonderful years, I formed a vision. I was sitting in the parking lot of the high school. My car was facing north. What I saw was a cornfield. It was the edge of town. It was in the line of expansion for a growing community. There was talk that the property I was looking at was going to be sold for yet another subdivision. I sat there pondering the plight of my struggling school district, a district that had run out of space. Gymnasium stages, locker rooms, storerooms, even libraries had been converted into classrooms. Some support staff were located in hallways with desks in cubbyholes. Confidence and money were hard to find. The community would not embrace another tax increase and too many negative attitudes hindered the good works and intentions of an outstanding School Board.

Sitting there, it dawned on me that what we needed was a new school. We needed a new middle school to allow relief for all the K-8 grade students. We could move the middle school students off their present campus and into a new building. The new building would be like a pressure relief valve for the entire district. And what better place than across the street from the high school, creating a new campus with endless possibilities. But it was *my* vision, and everyone knows that in order to make a vision come to fruition, it must be owned and embraced by the stakeholders.

Within weeks of that experience a group was formed to purchase the land. The Board began strategic planning with community engagement. Within five years and six referendums, and with a strong base of over three hundred supporters, the vision became reality. The school was built and the community celebrated many forms of success. One successful vision opened the doors to many others.

Was it my vision that started it all? Well, the answer is both yes and no. Yes, it was the focal point of a possible solution, and no, it had to become the collective vision of everyone in order to gain acceptance, support, and passion.

When the teacher in the Microsoft ad looks at her four students she visualizes four developing individuals. She sees four possibilitics: an artist, an athlete, a marine biologist, and a musician. Once she has her vision of what could be, she sets in motion the ingredients for success.

Teachers Change Lives 24/7

I imagine this teacher as one who encourages her students, suggests ways for them to experience their possibilities, and helps pave the way for their futures. She doesn't see four kids on a field trip. She sees four human beings needing help as they forge their way toward success. Her vision and passion will be the keys to opening new doors for these children. She will use those keys to help change their lives.

Do you have a vision? Can you see something that needs to be done and then help make it happen? Is your vision complicated or simple? Often, when I speak with teachers, I ask them to do two things when they return to their scheduled lives, to consider two simple yet profound requests.

First, I ask them to pick just *one student* and make a change in that student's life. Visualize that student succeeding in some arena. It might be developing the ability to cope with a family situation, or learning a trade, or embracing an art. It might be the development of an athletic skill, or the ability to read better, or discovering how to get along with peers or adults. My request to teachers is to find a student in need, visualize that student meeting that need, and then focus on ways to implement the vision.

The second request is to find *one area of personal weakness*. Focus on just one characteristic or trait that can be improved. It might be getting along better with a spouse, not being so negative when faced with the mundane responsibilities of the job, losing some weight, spending more time with a parent, learning how to teach more effectively, or bolstering church attendance.

A great way to improve yourself is through professional or personal development. Often we focus on just the professional development offered through the school or through a university. We even engage in some of the "canned" professional development offered by the school district, region, or state with a less than enthusiastic attitude. What a shame. Every experience is just as good as we make it.

I remember one well-respected teacher who walked out of an in-service presentation and said, "I didn't learn anything new today, but I reinforced a lot of things I am already doing, and it validated my efforts. That is a good feeling." She had the right attitude.

Another teacher commented, "I have never attended any workshop or institute where I didn't get at least one good idea to try." I believe her. I imagine she never went into one workshop or institute where she wasn't *looking* for one good idea to try!

Life is all about learning. Good teachers try to learn and improve at every venue possible. They expand their inventory of experiences and sift through ideas that can enhance, validate, or eliminate methods or procedures. They embrace professional or personal development opportunities. Just like the students they teach, they look for opportunities to learn.

I then ask teachers to write down both the student's name and their new personal goal on a piece of paper, maybe even in code to keep them personal, and keep the paper where they can see it every day. It becomes a reminder of their vision for change. What follows is for them to outline a plan, create steps to make this vision become reality, and make it happen. When it does happen, when they feel they have made substantial progress toward realizing their vision, replace that student with another, and replace the personal goal as well. Always have two, just two, workable visions in front of you. Make them realistic and doable.

Inch by inch, baby step by baby step, you can make things happen if you just see the end result and move toward it. Two manageable goals can give you the confidence to set bigger ones, to take on massive challenges, to change the world. Silly? Not for one minute, for what you see is what you get. See change and you will realize change.

What do *you* see when you look at your students? Do you remember that it is just as important to create opportunities to learn for yourself as it is for your students? What are your visions for the future?

When you look at your students, do you see them as what they are or what they could be? When you consider your own strengths and weaknesses, do you think of ways to improve yourself as a human, as a family member, and as a teacher? Are you able to create a vision and then turn it into reality?

I once had a friend who lost over 50 pounds. He looked terrific. I asked him how he did it. His answer has always impressed me. He said, "I visualized myself thinner and in better shape, and then I set a goal to lose one pound." He waited for my response, and then he said, I followed that with 49 more goal-setting experiences." His theory? Anyone can lose one pound, and if you can easily lose one pound, just repeat that process 49 more times to reach your vision.

One life can be changed if you break that life into manageable size chunks and work on it, one chunk at a time.

Create a vision, complete the vision, and what you have seen, is what you will get. It's a formula for changing lives.

◆ Develop a relationship with each student. Find out as much as you can about them, and about their families. Study their data folders. Talk to them. Take the time to see them in light of what you discover.

◆ Give kids a chance to grow. Give them responsibilities. Responsibilities are opportunities. Responsibilities give them dignity and maturity. Let them make mistakes, but be sure you are there to help them learn and grow from them. Then celebrate the growth!

◆ Communicate any good news with parents. Send personal letters, notes, or e-mails. Or phone messages home when a student does well on a test, raises his grades, or escapes from the D/F list. Don't just recognize the honor students; do it for all students.

◆ Use body language—erect posture, eye contact, and gestures—to send messages about behavioral expectations. Eye messages alone can sometimes defuse a possible disaster.

◆ Every classroom should have a "Welcome" sign on the door. A room number and the teacher's name are helpful too.

◆ Be careful about blood and other bodily secretions. But don't be phobic. Remember those training sessions about blood borne pathogens and follow the rules.

◆ Keep a Bible in your classroom, or any other religious book that you believe in. There is no law against it. It may come in handy.

◆ Don't wear one of those plastic penholders or pocket protectors in your shirt pocket. Kids will think you look like a nerd. Correctly.

◆ Never complain about school lunches—try feeding hundreds of kids on that budget! When you complain, others will follow. If you enjoy a meal, compliment the cook.

◆ Never have an empty bulletin board in your room. Consider it as free advertising space. Put up messages about the subject, character education, current events, school spirit, or a dozen other things that you want kids to know.

◆ Buy one of those bags or boxes you can hide in your desk drawer that laugh when you push a button. Once in a rare while push the button when the kids are working, studying, or taking a quiz. A good belly laugh is just about the best thing you can give another human being.

◆ If you don't love kids, love your job, and love the field of education, quit. Liking isn't good enough when it comes to children's lives.

◆ Go to the mall. Sit on a bench and watch people. See what well dressed men and women your age or slightly younger are wearing. If everybody else has shoes with laces and yours have Velcro straps, or all of the skirts you see fall at knee level and yours drags below your combat boots, consider getting a more modern wardrobe. You don't have to wear expensive clothes. But you will relate better if you wear appropriate and current styles.

◆ Teachers who look sloppy don't get the same respect from students as those who look professional. Looking like the kids is for the kids, not for teachers.

◆ Cleavage is something a meat cleaver provides. If you are showing cleavage, you are not properly dressed. Period.

◆ Never compare yourself with anything other than what you are, a college-educated, certified, professional educator. Carry that banner with dignity.

◆ Invite a non-educator friend to visit five classrooms and rate them according to how inviting, professional, comfortable, and exciting (you name the criteria) they are. Have one of the rooms be yours, but don't say which. You will get an honest evaluation of how well you have prepared your room for learning.

◆ Never tell a student a lie. Kids are living lie detectors. Lies will haunt you forever.

◆ If you feel like crying, cry. Teachers are humans too.

◆ Don't swear. Don't tolerate swearing. Don't apologize for not tolerating swearing. Be an example for others.

◆ Don't gossip. Never. Don't perpetuate or affirm or listen to gossip. Set yourself above it. Gossips lose credibility with everyone. You may not realize it now, but it is true.

◆ Don't yell. Students pay more attention if you talk normally or softly. Who likes to be yelled at? Don't do it at the schoolhouse or at your own house.

◆ If it is true, tell the kids that you are lucky to be a teacher, and that you love your job. If it isn't, find another one.

◆ Don't demand, ask. Don't interrupt, wait your turn. Don't whine, unless you bring cheese.

◆ Promote a child's imagination and initiative and discourage imitation and fear of failure. Do the same for yourself.

◆ Never run with scissors in hand and make sure you wear clean underwear in case you are in an accident! (The World Association of Mothers requires that this be listed.)

"I'd rather see a lesson than hear one any day. I'd rather you walk with me than to merely show the way."

Basketball coach Dale Brown
1956-

Chapter Fourteen

Be Unforgettable

At the beginning of every new school year it was always a goal of mine to get students off to a positive start. You already have read about my attitudes toward testing and assessments and how I loved to make them learning opportunities. I took this philosophy and incorporated it in a plan to start the year on an upswing.

The first test of the year was always a modified review of past knowledge. It was a way to get to know the kids, encourage them, and launch them on a new learning venture.

We would verbally review a number of basics in the subject matter. We talked about things they should already know but might need to review. I picked fundamental, basic, easy concepts. After this in-depth, often fun review, with lots of assurance that everyone was on the same page, I administered the first test. Granted, it was easy. It was designed to be doable by everyone but it wasn't meaningless and it served the valuable purpose of getting everyone over the summer brain drain and back on track. It was designed to get everyone off the starting blocks with a good grade and a positive attitude.

With it came a rather ambitious exercise. I contacted every family to report the grade and the experience. I called and left the good news on their answering machine.

What did I say?

"Hi, this is Jim Burgett, I am (Bob)'s science teacher. We took our first exam and Bob received an "A". I really look forward to working with Bob and invite you to contact me by calling the school with any questions or suggestions you might have. Thanks for loaning Bob to me for this year."

Sometimes I modified the script to match the person. What did all that accomplish? (1) An honest review of information needed for the coming year, (2) An exam designed to result in success, (3) A positive and encouraging family contact introducing me and asking for involvement, and (4) The creation of a comfortable learning environment.

Over the years many parents reported to me how unforgettable that simple phone message was. One Dad told me it was the only time anyone from the school had ever contacted him or his wife with something positive about their son. How sad, I thought. Another parent told me they thought about having the cassette tape with that message bronzed. I think (and hope) they were kidding.

I tried to be a positive, engaging teacher who actually loved working with every student, from the most challenging to the most gifted. I tried to foster an attitude of learning that fit their abilities and gave them hope and confidence.

I also tried to utilize the best practices from the best educators I knew, incorporating what I learned in professional development opportunities and through personal growth experiences.

Like you, I am human. I have bad and good days. Some of what I tried to do back-fired. Not every parent or student was in sync with my teaching methods or efforts. Not every administrator or peer thought that my way was the best way. But no matter what, I tried to forge ahead, learn from my mistakes, and do better. My passion for teaching never waned, nor has it yet. My love for kids has always been foremost in my mind, and as recently as last night when I met with three high school boys as part of our church disciple group. I made an effort to understand their needs and was eager to visualize a way to help them achieve their goals.

If you have taken this book journey with me, thank you. Along the way we've met many wonderful examples of life changers. You've read hundreds of ideas and suggestions that educators who make a difference have made available for all of us. You've heard about the importance of balancing your home life with your school life. And you have embraced some essential concepts that just might help you become unforgettable.

Need I remind you that the Evil Witch substitute and Mrs. Breckenridge were as unforgettable as were Mr. Ruggles, Mr. B, and the other positive beacons mentioned on these pages.

I'm hoping that you too will be unforgettable in a positive, wonderful way. My hope is that your students, when talking to their children, will tell tales about you full of hope, of what they learned, and of compassion, all shared with great fondness. I hope they will remember you as a person who not only led them to learning, but did it with passion and love.

Last night one of the boys in my group was lamenting the fact that a certain high school English teacher was dismissed from the district due to financial cuts. She was a mature lady and an experienced teacher who had only been in our community for a few years and had not yet achieved job-saving tenure. It was a painful situation for the district and for the kids.

One of the boys said, "I really liked her. She came to you when she thought you were struggling with the work. She loved being a teacher. She treated everyone the same way, fairly. She knew her stuff and made it fun." Words from a 16-year-old high school junior.

And then he spontaneously said, "I don't think I will ever forget her."

That touched my heart because that's the goal. That's the journey.

◆ You are a teacher. You do change lives. You set examples. You model what is right.

Your job isn't easy but it pays dividends far greater than any paycheck. You are blessed. Cherish the privilege.

You have been given one of the most awesome responsibilities on the face of the earth, that of teaching something to someone for life. You have a singular opportunity to be unforgettable in your own way multiplied by a hundred or many thousand times—to change young lives 24/7 forever.

Thank you for reading my book. I would love to hear what you think. Please email me at jburgett@burgettgroup.com.

And Keep Changing Lives.

Jim

Bibliography

Blanchard, K., S. Johnson, and E. Harvey, *The One-Minute Manager*. New York: William Morrow, 1981.

Blanchard, K., and N.V. Peale, *The Power of Ethical Management*. New York: William Morrow, 1988.

Blanchard, K., B. Hybels, and P. Hodges, *Leadership by the Book*. New York: William Morrow, 1999.

Blase, Joseph, and Kirby, Peggy C., *Bringing Out the Best in Teachers*. Thousand Oaks, CA: Corwin Pess, Inc., 2000.

Bluestein, Jane, *Mentors, Masters and Mrs. MacGregor*. Deerfield Beach, FL: Health Communications, Inc., 1995.

Bolman, Lee G., and Terrence E. Deal, *Leading With Soul*. San Francisco: Jossey-Bass Inc., 1995.

Connors, Neila A., *If You Don't Feed the Teachers They Eat the Students.* Nashville: Incentive Publications, 2000.

Harvey, E., and A. Lucia, *Walk the Talk—and Get the Results You Want*. Dallas: Performance Publishing Co., 1995

Jones, Laurie, *Jesus CEO—Using Ancient Wisdom for Visionary Leadership*. New York: Hyperion, 1995.

Lewis, J., Jr., *Implementing Total Quality in Education to Produce Great Schools*. Westbury, NY: National Center to Save Our Schools, 1993.

Maxwell, J., *Failing Forward*. Nashville: Thomas Nelson, 2000.

Maxwell, J., *The 21 Indispensable Qualities of a Leader*. Nashville: Thomas Nelson, 1999.

Maxwell, J., *The 21 Most Powerful Minutes in a Leader's Day*. Nashville: Thomas Nelson, 2000.

Morris, Rick, *Class Cards*. San Diego, CA: New Management, 2001.

Novak, Dori, *Help! It's An Indoor Recess Day*. Thousand Oaks, CA: Corwin Press, Inc., 2000.

Oakes, J., and M. Lipton, *Teaching to Change the World*. Boston: McGraw-Hill, 1999.

Peale, N.V., *The Power of Positive Thinking*. New York: Prentice-Hall, 1952.

Peterson, Art, *Teachers—A Survival Guide for the Grownup in the Classroom*. New York: Penguin Books, 1985.

Phillips, D.T., *Lincoln on Leadership*. New York: Warner Books, 1992.

Rosborg, J., Max McGee, and J. Burgett, *What Every Superintendent and Principal Needs to Know*. Santa Maria, CA: Education Communication Unlimited, 2003.

Strike, K.A., E.J. Haller, and J.F. Soltis, *The Ethics of School Administration*. New York: Teachers College Press, 1988.

Tileston, Donna W., *10 Best Teaching Practices*. Thousand Oaks, CA: Corwin Press, Inc., 2000.

Urban, Hal*, Life's Greatest Lessons—20 Things That Matter*. New York: Fireside, 2003.

Wooden, John, and Steve Jamison, *My Personal Best*. New York: McGraw-Hill, 2004.

Wright, Esther, *Good Morning Class—I Love You!* Torrance, CA: Jalmar Press, 1989.

Ziglar, Zig, *See You at the Top*. 3rd ed. Gretna, LA: Pelican Publishing Company, 1978.

Index

Teachers Change Lives 24/7

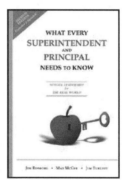